NWA

TW GHT

Longman
is an imprint of

PEARSON

YORK
PRESS

YORK PRESS
322 Old Brompton Road, London SW5 9JH

PEARSON EDUCATION LIMITED
Edinburgh Gate, Harlow,
Essex CM20 2JE, United Kingdom

Associated companies, branches and representatives throughout the world

First published 2000
This new and fully revised edition 2013

10 9 8 7 6 5 4 3 2 1

ISBN 978–1–4479–4888–9

Illustration on page 9 by Neil Gower
Phototypeset by Border Consultants
Printed in Italy

Photo credits:

© INTERFOTO/Alamy for page 6 top / © P. Spiro/Alamy for page 6 bottom / ©iStockphoto.com/kparis for page 7 bottom / Lowe R. Llaguno/Shutterstock.com for page 8 / Chris Mullins/Shutterstock.com for page 10 / Graham Taylor Photography/Shutterstock.com for page 11 top / Elena Vasilchenko/Shutterstock.com for page 11 bottom / Danilo Ascione/Shutterstock.com for page 12 / StanOd/Shutterstock.com for page 13 / Johann Helgason/Shutterstock.com for page 15 / ©iStockphoto.com/ivkuzmin for page 16 top / ©iStockphoto.com/EugenioCini for page 16 bottom / Dasha Petrenko/Shutterstock.com for page 18 / sam100/Shutterstock.com for page 19 top / Dan Kosmayer/Shutterstock.com for page 19 bottom / Robert Anthony/Shutterstock.com for page 21 / ukmooney/Shutterstock.com for page 22 middle / Fotocrisis/Shutterstock.com for page 22 bottom / Elnur/Shutterstock.com for page 23 / ollyy/Shutterstock.com for page 24 / ©iStockphoto.com/JaniceRichard for page 25 top / Aprilphoto/Shutterstock.com for page 26 / Elnur/Shutterstock.com for page 27 / Piotr Neffe/Shutterstock.com for page 28 / alersandr hunta/Shutterstock.com for page 29 / Colin Anderson/Getty Images for page 30 / Hintau Aliaksei/Shutterstock.com for page 31 / Sergey_Bogomyako/Shutterstock.com for page 32 top / DEA/A. DE GREGORIO/Getty Images for page 32 bottom / Mana Photo/Shutterstock.com for page 33 top / Vasaleks/Shutterstock.com for page 33 bottom / sam100/Shutterstock.com for page 34 / Galushko Sergey/Shutterstock.com for page 35 / LiliGraphie/Shutterstock.com for page 36 / Dasha Petrenko/Shutterstock.com for page 37 / courtyardpix/Shutterstock.com for page 38 top / ©iStockphoto.com/NoDerog for page 38 bottom / AndyTu/Shutterstock.com for page 39 / Zoltan Pataki/Shutterstock.com for page 40 / Anneka/Shutterstock.com for page 42 top / © Sandro Vannini/CORBIS for page 42 bottom / Markus Gann/Shutterstock.com for page 43 / © David Crausby/Alamy for page 45 top / Eduard Harkonen/Shutterstock.com for page 45 bottom / Anthro/Shutterstock.com for page 46 / Julia Remezova/Shutterstock.com for page 47 / OPIS Zagreb/Shutterstock.com for page 48 / Owain Kirby/Getty Images for page 49 top / Offscreen/Shutterstock.com for page 49 bottom / ollyy/Shutterstock.com for page 50 / Africa Studio/Shutterstock.com for page 51 middle / karnizz/Shutterstock.com for page 51 bottom / ©iStockphoto.com/PaoloGaetano for page 52 / ©iStockphoto.com/kikkerdirk for page 53 top / tommaso lizzul/Shutterstock.com for page 53 bottom / PCHT/Shutterstock.com for page 54 / ARCANGELO/Shutterstock.com for page 55 top / ©iStockphoto.com/mujdatuzel for page 55 bottom / Colin Anderson/ Getty Images for page 56 top / Avesun/Shutterstock.com for page 56 middle / ©iStockphoto.com/JohnnyGreig for page 57 / ©iStockphoto.com/caracterdesign for page 58 / Dasha Petrenko/Shutterstock.com for page 59 / sam100/Shutterstock.com for page 60 top / Dima Sobko/Shutterstock.com for page 60 bottom / Volodymyr Burdiak/Shutterstock.com for page 61 / courtyardpix/ Shutterstock.com for page 62 top / ©iStockphoto.com/ptaxa for page 62 bottom / brem stocker/Shutterstock.com for page 63 / ©iStockphoto.com/kemter for page 64 / iofoto/Shutterstock.com for page 65 / ollyy/Shutterstock.com for page 66 / Markus Gann/Shutterstock.com for page 67 / Anna-Mari West/Shutterstock.com for page 68 / Rafal Olechowski/Shutterstock.com for page 69 middle / Brian A Jackson/Shutterstock.com for page 69 bottom / senticus/Shutterstock.com for page 70 top / Yuttasak Jannarong/Shutterstock.com for page 70 bottom / leungchopan/Shutterstock.com for page 71 / Mark Hamilton/Getty Images for page 72 top / Gromovataya/Shutterstock.com for page 72 bottom / Claudio Divizia/Shutterstock.com for page 73 top / Studio 37/Shutterstock.com for page 73 bottom / Travel Ink/Getty Images for page 74 top / Netfalls – Remy Musser/Shutterstock.com for page 74 bottom / Dario Sabljak/Shutterstock.com for page 76 / Bplanet/Shutterstock.com for page 77 top / ©iStockphoto.com/ peanut8481 for page 77 bottom / Goran Bogicevic/Shutterstock.com for page 78 / Samot/Shutterstock.com for page 79 / SusaZoom/Shutterstock.com for page 80 top / valzan/Shutterstock.com for page 80 bottom / © Lebrecht Music and Arts Photo Library/Alamy for page 81 / ktdesign/Shutterstock.com for page 82 / slavapolo/Shutterstock.com for page 83 / © Maurice Savage/Alamy for page 85 top / Gts/Shutterstock.com for page 85 bottom / Arsgera/Shutterstock.com for page 86 top / Image Source/Getty Images for page 86 middle / Iakov Kalinin/Shutterstock.com for page 87 / ©iStockphoto.com/Goldfaery for page 101 / ©iStockphoto.com/skynesher for page 103

CONTENTS

PART FIVE: CONTEXTS AND CRITICAL DEBATES

PART SIX: GRADE BOOSTER

ESSENTIAL STUDY TOOLS

HOW TO STUDY *TWELFTH NIGHT*

These Notes can be used in a range of ways to help you read, study and (where relevant) revise for your exam or assessment.

READING THE PLAY

Read the play once, fairly quickly, for pleasure. This will give you a good sense of the overarching shape of the plot, and a good feel for the highs and lows of the action, the pace and style, and the sequence in which information is withheld or revealed. You could ask yourself:

- How do individual characters change or develop? How do my own responses to them change?
- How does Shakespeare allow the audience to see into the minds and motives of the characters? Does he use **asides**, **soliloquies** or other dramatic devices, for example?
- What sort of language do different characters use? Does Shakespeare use **imagery**, or recurring **motifs** or **symbols**?
- Are the events presented chronologically, or is the time scheme altered in some way?
- What impression does the setting, in Illyria, make on my reading and response to the play?
- How could the play be presented on the stage in different ways? How could different types of performance affect the audience's interpretation of the play?

On your second reading, make detailed notes around the key areas highlighted above and in the Assessment Objectives, such as form, language, structure (AO2), links and connections to other texts (AO3) and the context/background for the play (AO4). These may seem quite demanding, but these Notes will suggest particular elements to explore or jot down.

INTERPRETING OR CRITIQUING THE PLAY

Although it's not helpful to think in terms of the play being 'good' or 'bad', you should consider the different ways the play can be read. How have critics responded to it? Do their views match yours – or do you take a different viewpoint? Are there different ways you can interpret specific events, characters or settings? This is a key aspect in AO3, and it can be helpful to keep a log of your responses and the various perspectives which are expressed both by established critics, but also by classmates, your teacher, or other readers.

REFERENCES AND SOURCES

You will be expected to draw on critics' or reviewers' comments, and refer to relevant literary or historical sources that might have influenced Shakespeare or his contemporaries. Make sure you make accurate, clear notes of writers or sources you have used, for example noting down titles of works, authors' names, website addresses, dates, etc. You may not have to reference all these things when you respond to a text, but knowing the source of your information will allow you to go back to it – and to check its accuracy and relevance.

REVISING FOR AND RESPONDING TO AN ASSESSED TASK OR EXAM QUESTION

The structure and the contents of these Notes are designed to give you relevant information or ideas to answer tasks you have been set. First, work out the key words or ideas from the task (for example, 'form', 'Act I', 'Malvolio', etc.), then read the parts of the Notes that relate to these terms or words, selecting what is useful for revision or written response. Then, turn to **Part Six: Grade Booster** for help in formulating your actual response.

CONTEXT **A04**

Twelfth Night was first printed in 1623, seven years after Shakespeare's death in 1616, as part of the first collected edition of his works, *Mr William Shakespeares Comedies, Tragedies, & Histories*, known as the First Folio. In the contents page of this edition it is listed under 'Comedies' and given its full title 'Twelfth Night, or What You Will'. All modern editions of the play, including *The New Cambridge Shakespeare* text edited by Elizabeth Story Donno to which these Notes refer, are derived from this first publication.

TWELFTH NIGHT IN CONTEXT

SHAKESPEARE'S LIFE AND TIMES

1564	William Shakespeare born in Stratford-upon-Avon (date of birth unknown, baptised 26 April)
1582	Shakespeare marries Anne Hathaway; in 1583 their daughter, Susanna, is born, followed by their twins, Hamnet and Judith, in 1585
1592	Recorded as being a London actor and an 'upstart crow'
1592–4	Writes *The Comedy of Errors*
1595 (pre-)	*The Two Gentlemen of Verona*, *The Taming of the Shrew* and *Love's Labour's Lost* probably written
1596–8	Death of twin son, Hamnet; first performance, *The Merchant of Venice*
1600	*A Midsummer Night's Dream, Much Ado about Nothing* and *The Merchant of Venice* printed in quartos
1600–2	*Twelfth Night* written
1613	Globe Theatre burns down
1616	Death of William Shakespeare
1623	First Folio of Shakespeare's works

CHECK THE BOOK **A03**

The Introduction to *The New Cambridge Shakespeare* edition gives an excellent summary of the play's stage history and some of the famous productions (pp. 36–52).

EARLY STAGING

Twelfth Night was probably written in late 1600–1, and had its first performance in 1601. Attempts to suggest it was premièred at Elizabeth's court on twelfth night (6 January, the final day of Christmas festivities) in 1601 are fanciful (see **Part Three: Themes**), although Shakespeare may have taken the name of his lovesick Duke from Elizabeth's Italian guest on that occasion, the young nobleman Don Virginio Orsino, Duke of Bracchiano. We do know that it was performed at the Middle Temple (see photo) in February 1602, the feast of Candlemas, because a law student John Manningham wrote in his diary:

At our feast we had a play called *Twelfth Night, or What You Will*, much like *The Comedy of Errors* or *Menaechmi* in Plautus, but most like and near to that in Italian called *Inganni* [see **Part Five: Literary Background**]. A good practice in it to make the steward believe his lady widow was in love with him, by counterfeiting a letter as from his lady, in general terms telling him what she liked best in him, and prescribing his gesture in smiling, his

apparel, etc., and then when he came to practise, making him believe they took him to be mad.

Manningham's account is interesting in its exclusive stress on the Malvolio plot, giving an indication of what one early spectator found most engaging about the play (see **Part Five: Critical Debates**).

STUDY FOCUS: MARS AND VENUS? **A02**

An episode of the American tabloid talk-show hosted by Jerry Springer was entitled 'My boyfriend is a girl', and featured women who maintained they had been unaware that their dates were not male after all. In *Twelfth Night* we can find the same interest in girls dressed as boys and the erotic games this seems to involve. By making Viola's appearance identical with her male twin, however, Shakespeare can focus not simply on the erotic interplay, but also on the emotional psychology of the individual characters. One question to consider is whether the cross-dressing convention ultimately confirms or undermines our expectations of male and female behaviour. Does its use with Viola in *Twelfth Night* perhaps show what modern research is now revealing (see, for example, the *Journal of Personality and Social Psychology* 2013) that, in terms of personality traits, there is much overlap between men and women and that no trait can be designated simply 'male' or 'female'? Characters who begin by believing otherwise, such as Orsino, who impotently rages, 'There is no woman's sides/ Can bide the beating of so strong a passion/ As love doth give my heart' (II.4.89–91), could be seen to come to such a realisation through their encounter with Viola as Cesario. Sir Andrew is punished after trying to behave as the aggressive male, a role for which he is totally unsuited, and it is Sebastian, after all, whom we see in tears following the shipwreck and close to them when restored to his twin sister, not Viola.

WHAT YOU WILL

If the classic romantic comedy could be summarised as girl meets boy and falls in love, *Twelfth Night* offers a beguiling range of variations on this theme: girl falls in love with girl dressed as boy, boy falls for girl dressed as boy, girl dressed as boy makes herself attractive to girl and boy. What this shows is that these titillating combinations are not just a modern whim. In this context, the play's subtitle, 'What You Will', becomes laden with innuendo, a version of 'anything goes'.

CHECK THE FILM **A03**

An ongoing interest in gender roles, cross-dressing and sexuality can be seen in plays such as *One Man Two Guvnors* (2011), itself derived from Goldoni's *The Servant of Two Masters* (1743), and Martin Crimp's *The False Servant* (2004, translated from Marivaux's *La Fausse Suivante*, 1724). It can also be seen in films, from *Sylvia Scarlett* (1935) and *Some Like It Hot* (1959) via *Tootsie* (1982) and *Mrs Doubtfire* (1993) to *The Crying Game* (1992).

'A MOST EXTRACTING FRENZY'

The play shows a number of instances of love, from selfless to selfish, from altruistic to narcissistic. It is concerned with unrequited and unexpected love. It also has a vein of cruelty in which the audience is uncomfortably implicated. There is a hectic, slightly desperate feeling about the action, as if the characters are running out of options, hence the hurry to get married and wrap everything up at the end. As Olivia says, it is 'A most extracting frenzy' (V.1.265). It is a comedy with a melancholy aftertaste, a temporary umbrella against the wintry rain that Feste sings of in his final song, and so it is perhaps not surprising that *Twelfth Night* is often identified as Shakespeare's last comedy, shading into the darker mood of the so-called 'problem plays' and the great tragedies.

THE SETTING

Twelfth Night is set in Illyria, a name which evokes a romantic atmosphere with its suggestions of lyrical delirium. Its festive, topsy-turvy world is a curious mixture of revelry and reverie, laughter and melancholy in which mayhem rules. Music begins and ends the play and is an essential means by which the play conveys feelings of joy and sadness for the characters and audience. Illyria has therefore been readily adaptable to various historical and modern contexts. In a play which is full of references to the theatre and which has cross-dressing as its major plot device, however, it is helpful to be aware of the Elizabethan stage practice of boys playing women. In this respect, although *Twelfth Night* is often set in a recent or modern period, the Elizabethan setting of the all-male Globe production with the actor Mark Rylance (2012) provided new and revealing insights into the world of the play.

CHECK THE FILM A03

Notable film and television versions include the BBC TV production (1981), Kenneth Branagh's for Channel 4 (1988) and Trevor Nunn's film (1996).

STUDY FOCUS: *TWELFTH NIGHT* IN PERFORMANCE A04

Twelfth Night, with its combination of light and dark elements, provokes a combination of responses, as the representatives of order and misrule battle it out for final supremacy in one of Shakespeare's most popular plays, named after the last day of the Christmas festivities. The literary richness of the text is evident from Orsino's opening words, but it is first and foremost a work of theatre. Study of the text should be informed, if at all possible, by experiencing it in performance, though it is worth remembering that any production will be the result of choices and decisions made by the directors and actors and so will only ever be a partial realisation of the possibilities it offers.

CHARACTERS IN *TWELFTH NIGHT*

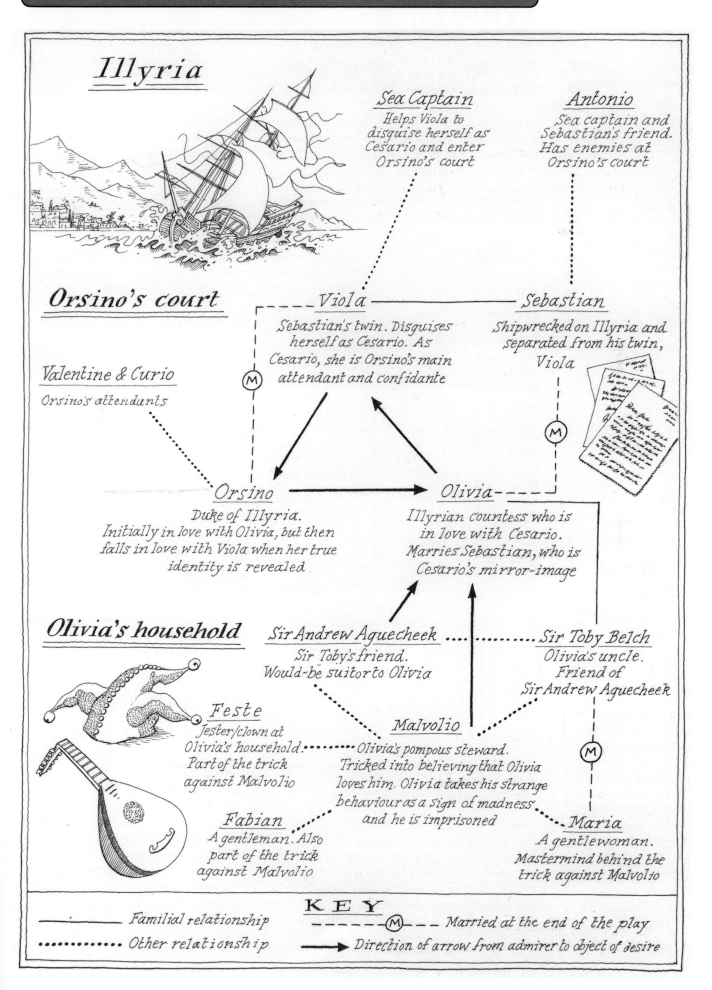

Illyria

Sea Captain
Helps Viola to disguise herself as Cesario and enter Orsino's court

Antonio
Sea captain and Sebastian's friend. Has enemies at Orsino's court

Orsino's court

Valentine & Curio
Orsino's attendants

Viola
Sebastian's twin. Disguises herself as Cesario. As Cesario, she is Orsino's main attendant and confidante

Sebastian
Shipwrecked on Illyria and separated from his twin, Viola

Orsino
Duke of Illyria. Initially in love with Olivia, but then falls in love with Viola when her true identity is revealed

Olivia
Illyrian countess who is in love with Cesario. Marries Sebastian, who is Cesario's mirror-image

Olivia's household

Sir Andrew Aguecheek
Sir Toby's friend. Would-be suitor to Olivia

Sir Toby Belch
Olivia's uncle. Friend of Sir Andrew Aguecheek

Feste
Jester/clown at Olivia's household. Part of the trick against Malvolio

Malvolio
Olivia's pompous steward. Tricked into believing that Olivia loves him. Olivia takes his strange behaviour as a sign of madness and he is imprisoned

Fabian
A gentleman. Also part of the trick against Malvolio

Maria
A gentlewoman. Mastermind behind the trick against Malvolio

KEY

——— Familial relationship

············ Other relationship

– – –Ⓜ– – – Married at the end of the play

———▶ Direction of arrow from admirer to object of desire

SYNOPSIS

SEA OF LOVE

Orsino, the Duke of Illyria, is in love with the Countess Olivia, who does not return his affections and is in long mourning for her dead brother. Viola is shipwrecked on the coast of Illyria, in a storm in which she believes her twin brother Sebastian has drowned. Disguising herself in male clothes, she goes to work for Orsino as a page, under the name Cesario, and quickly becomes his firm favourite. Orsino sends his young page as a go-between to Olivia. The Countess receives Cesario and quickly falls in love with him. Viola's predicament is complicated by her own love for Orsino.

DEVOTION AND DANGER

Sebastian is rescued by Antonio, a sea captain, and sets off for Orsino's court. Antonio is devoted to Sebastian and, despite being a wanted man in Illyria, resolves to follow him and act as his servant. When they meet again later, Antonio lends Sebastian his purse, but lies low while Sebastian views the town.

FOOLING

Meanwhile, Olivia's drunken uncle Sir Toby Belch, her lady-in-waiting Maria and her would-be suitor Sir Andrew Aguecheek, together with her servant Fabian and her fool Feste, have hatched a plot against her steward Malvolio, who interrupted their late-night carousing. Maria fakes Olivia's handwriting in a letter to Malvolio which tells him his mistress is in love with him, and that she wishes him to smile and wear yellow stockings and cross-garters. Malvolio falls for the trick. For more sport, Sir Toby and Fabian arrange a duel between Sir Andrew and Cesario, the knight's supposed 'rival' for the hand of Olivia.

MADNESS

Malvolio follows the instructions of the letter and Olivia thinks him mad. The members of her household continue the 'jest' by imprisoning him in a dark room as a lunatic, where Feste later pretends to be a priest to torment him. Antonio, mistaking Viola for Sebastian, halts the duel between her and Sir Andrew, and is arrested by officers for an old offence against the state. He asks for the return of his purse and when Viola professes not to know him rails at the apparent betrayal. Viola departs, but Sir Toby, Fabian and Sir Andrew follow her. They come across Sebastian and, mistaken for Cesario, he becomes embroiled in the arranged duel with Sir Andrew. Olivia interrupts the fight and so meets Sebastian, whom she also believes to be Cesario. Sebastian is attracted to her and the Countess hastily arranges their betrothal of marriage.

GRADE BOOSTER **A02**

Commentators have taken different positions regarding the idea of character stereotypes in the play. Much contemporary humour still plays with them. Does Shakespeare's comedy confirm or dissolve them? As you explore the play, decide for yourself and justify your views using the evidence of the words and actions of the characters.

REUNION

Orsino and Cesario arrive at Olivia's house. Antonio is brought before the Duke and accuses his seemingly false companion of ingratitude. Olivia appears, but she continues to reject Orsino's love and when she claims Cesario as her husband, Orsino rages at his apparently dishonest page. Sir Toby and Sir Andrew both enter, wounded by Sebastian, and depart, with Sir Toby berating his companion. When Sebastian appears, the twins are restored to each other and their true identities are revealed. Feste delivers a letter from Malvolio and Olivia orders his release, but Malvolio will not be reconciled and departs threatening revenge. Sir Toby has married Maria. Orsino realises his love for Viola and resolves to marry her. Feste is left alone to sing a melancholy song.

ACT I SCENE 1

SUMMARY

- Orsino, Duke of Illyria, expresses his deep love for Olivia, a countess.
- Orsino's servant Valentine returns from Olivia's household where Orsino's courtship has been rejected.
- Valentine tells Orsino that Olivia will remain in mourning for her dead brother for seven years.

ANALYSIS

IS IT LOVE?

The first scene is important in establishing the status of Orsino's love for Olivia. It seems a rather self-indulgent emotion, which is less about her as an individual and more the result of his idealised image of her. His love at first sight (lines 20–2) offers a romanticised view of her (see **Part Three: Characters**), and his language in this scene is often conventional, even **clichéd**. This suggestion may be strengthened by the fact that he does not mention Olivia by name until nearly the end of his first speech about his love for her.

Another interpretation, however, is that his language indicates his capacity for strong feeling and a responsiveness to music, often a positive feature of Shakespeare's characters. What might be criticised as extravagance could be interpreted as passion and a zest and vigour for life's pleasures.

STUDY FOCUS: APPETITE AND EXCESS · A02

Orsino's language through the scene is characterised by excess, and so introduces an important theme of the play (see **Part Three: Themes**, on **Excess**). Like the young Romeo who is in love with Rosaline before he sees Juliet in the earlier play *Romeo and Juliet*, there is a suggestion in the **hyperbole** of his language that he is in love with the sensation of being in love. His love is discussed in terms of appetite – another important theme of the play. That this is not only, or primarily, a romantic, spiritual form of love is stressed by the vivid **image** of his consuming physical desires, 'like fell and cruel hounds' (lines 22–4): the reference is to the legend of Actaeon, a huntsman who was turned into a deer and torn to pieces by his hounds as a punishment for glimpsing the virginal goddess Diana bathing. Where else does Orsino refer to the body in this scene?

ORSINO AND OLIVIA

In this romantic atmosphere, it is highly appropriate that the go-between for Orsino and Olivia should be called Valentine. Our first impressions of Olivia, via his report, also identify her as a character of strong emotions. While she and Orsino could be seen as opposites, he confining himself in thoughts of love, she with grief, we might also think that they are rather similar, single-minded personalities. The length of her mourning for her brother, the severity of her veiled demeanour and her continual weeping – 'And water once a day her chamber round/ With eye-offending brine' (lines 29–30) – all suggest a woman of intense passions. In establishing two such extreme characters, the play arouses our curiosity and interest about how events will unfold.

KEY QUOTATION: ACT I SCENE 1 `A01`

Orsino opens the play, stating: 'If music be the food of love, play on;/ Give me excess of it, that surfeiting,/ The appetite may sicken and so die!' (lines 1–3)

- Orsino says he wants an excess of music to kill his appetite for love.
- He could also be indulging his love of being in love.
- Music begins and ends the play and works in different ways through the plot.
- Orsino's opening statement could be seen to contain within it the movement of the whole play which, like a party, goes from appetite, to feasting and revelry and then to the after-effects.

GLOSSARY

4	**dying fall**	musical cadence which falls to its resolution
9	**quick**	keen
12	**pitch**	height, excellence
15	**high fantastica**	extremely imaginative
17	**hart**	deer, with a pun on 'heart'
22	**fell**	savage
26	**element**	sky
27	**ample**	full
28	**cloistress**	nun
30	**season**	preserve
33	**frame**	construction
35	**shaft**	Cupid's arrow
37	**liver, brain, and heart**	Renaissance thought held these organs to be the centre of the passions, judgements and sentiments

GRADE BOOSTER `A02`

Orsino's language here, including extended **metaphors** (conceits), **similes**, **apostrophe**, 'O spirit of love, how quick and fresh art thou' (line 9), and **paradox**, 'Stealing and giving odour' (line 7), is influenced by the vogue for love **sonnets** following the popularity of the Italian poet **Petrarch** and those English writers influenced by him. Can you find examples of metaphors and similes in Orsino's opening speech? What do they suggest about his attitude to love and to Olivia?

ACT I SCENE 2

SUMMARY

In Trevor Nunn's film of the play (1996), a prologue tells us that Messaline, the country where Viola was born, is at war with Illyria, which is immediately represented as a sinister police state. It is made clear that Viola's actions are motivated by fear, as she and her fellow survivors flee into some caves in the cliff when a menacing squad of black-uniformed horsemen gallop along the beach.

- Viola has been in a shipwreck and is cast up on the Illyrian coast with the Captain.
- She fears her twin brother Sebastian is drowned, but the Captain gives her hope that Sebastian survived.
- The Captain tells Viola of Orsino's unrequited love for Olivia and of Olivia's grief over the death of her brother.
- Viola has heard her father mention Orsino and decides to disguise herself as a eunuch and serve Orsino.

ANALYSIS

SEA AND SALTWATER

Viola's arrival by water makes literal two **images** from the previous scene: the sea of love in Orsino's first speech (line 11), and Olivia's saltwater tears or 'brine' (line 30), and so her mediating role between them is subtly suggested. She also shares with Olivia the loss of a brother, and this sense of emotional identification may explain her exclamation 'O that I served that lady' (line 42). Her brisk question, 'What country, friends, is this?' (line 1), suggests that she is resourceful, thinking about their situation and what is to be done rather than succumbing to fatigue or despair or grief. In this she is immediately contrasted with our initial image of Orsino and Olivia, both of whom are presented as static, passively responding rather than actively instigating.

Eunuchs, castrated males, had a powerful position in the Ottoman court, and in oriental harems they might be attended by mutes (see line 62). Mutes were often physically powerful men who, by virtue of their silence, had access to court secrets and who sometimes acted as executioners.

STUDY FOCUS: IN DISGUISE A02

It is not immediately clear why Viola decides to dress herself as a eunuch. There is a hint at her compatibility with Orsino in her abilities in music – the comfort he demands at the beginning of the play. But, if her father knew Orsino, why does she not ask for the Duke's hospitality after her ordeal? Why does she not tell of her 'estate' (line 44) – both social and emotional – and gain a welcome suitable to her status? Rather, Viola chooses 'disguise' and to 'conceal'. Perhaps, following the trauma of the shipwreck and her delivery into a strange country, Viola adopts male clothing as some kind of physical, social or psychological protection, just as previous Shakespearean heroines such as Rosalind in *As You Like It* and Julia in *The Two Gentlemen of Verona* had done before. Whatever the reason, her decision drives much of the plot from this point on and she is never seen in female attire again. Consider how Viola's disguise affects the world of Illyria.

GLOSSARY

4	**Elysium**	the heaven of classical mythology
5	**Perchance**	perhaps
6	**perchance**	here the **pun** plays on the previous sense, and means 'only by chance'
15	**Arion**	a Greek musician who, according to mythology, was saved from the sea by a dolphin enchanted by his singing
32	**murmur**	rumour
44	**compass**	achieve
47	**behaviour**	outward appearance
61	**wit**	plan, design

ACT I SCENE 3

SUMMARY

- Sir Toby Belch, uncle to Olivia, complains to her attendant Maria about his niece's behaviour.
- Maria advises him to keep his drinking and revelry under control.
- They discuss Sir Toby's companion Sir Andrew Aguecheek, who is trying to woo Olivia.
- When Aguecheek appears, his vanity and literal-mindedness are made the butt of the others' bawdiness and quick wits.
- Sir Toby needs Sir Andrew's money and so encourages him in his love for Olivia and in the idea that he is an excellent dancer.
- They leave with Sir Andrew capering to Sir Toby's command.

ANALYSIS

A DOUBLE ACT

Like Orsino and Olivia in the first scene, Sir Toby is **characterised** by excess. He roundly refuses Maria's sensible remark about self-restraint: 'you must confine yourself within the modest limits of order' (lines 6–7). He is devoted to self-gratification without much thought for others, but he is not the only character in the play who could be described this way. Sir Toby's motivations are selfish, fleshly ones. He lives to enjoy drinking and merrymaking, and can be seen as the embodiment of the play's festive, comic energies (see **Part Three: Themes**, on **Twelfth Night**). Sir Andrew Aguecheek is clearly wealthy and claims to be well educated, but, as Maria says, is 'a very fool' (line 19), and this diagnosis is confirmed when he fails to understand Sir Toby's encouragement 'accost' (line 40, a naval term, meaning to go alongside), and takes it for Maria's name. He and Sir Andrew, often played as a comic double act of fat man/thin man, are popular with audiences as an earthy contrast to the elevated emotions and expressions of the two noble households of Orsino and Olivia.

STUDY FOCUS: BAWDY BANTER

A01

Act I Scene 3 provides another contrast in characters and language. It is in prose rather than the **blank verse** of the previous two scenes and the word play is of a bantering, bawdy style. For example, when Sir Andrew asks if his hair suits him, Sir Toby replies, with a clear sexual reference, 'Excellent; it hangs like flax on a distaff; and I hope to see a huswife take thee between her legs and spin it off' (lines 84–5). A 'huswife' might be a prostitute, and this joke is about venereal disease, which was thought to cause baldness. That the jokes may be lost on Sir Andrew only adds to the audience's enjoyment. What other examples are there of bawdy jokes in this scene and what effect do they have on the mood of the play?

GLOSSARY

5	**except, before excepted**	a legalism, meaning to exclude what has already been excluded
6–7	**modest limits of order**	bounds of reasonable behaviour
9	**and**	if
16	**tall**	courageous (as well as of height)

GRADE BOOSTER **A02**

Shakespeare uses the names of the two knights as jokes to announce their comic function in the play and to signify character traits. Both names refer to the body: Sir Toby Belch has an obvious link, but Aguecheek is made from 'ague' (a fever) and 'cheek' (the face or buttocks). Identify at least two other characters who have meaningful names, and explain what they suggest.

GLOSSARY continued

18	**three thousand ducats**	intended to register that Sir Andrew has a substantial income
19	**have but ... ducats**	he'll spend the lot in a year
19	**very**	complete
22	**without book**	by memory
24	**natural**	foolish
26	**gust**	relish
28	**substractors**	detractors
33	**coistrill**	knave, low person

34	**parish top**	spinning top
	Castiliano vulgo	a much-discussed phrase, with 'Speak of the devil' probably its nearest equivalent
38	**shrew**	probably a reference to Maria's small size, but the other association of shrew – as ill-tempered woman – means it is hardly complimentary
42	**chambermaid**	lady-in-waiting
54	**in hand**	to deal with
56	**Marry**	mild oath, originally 'By Mary'
57	**thought is free**	a stock response to the question 'Do you think I'm a fool?'
58	**buttery bar**	serving counter in a liquor store-room. Most performances make this a reference to Maria's breasts
60	**dry**	thirsty, perhaps with an association of 'withered' or impotent
61–2	**keep my hand dry**	'Fools have wit enough to keep themselves out of the rain' was a proverb
63	**dry**	both 'not wet' and '**ironic**'
67	**canary**	sweet wine
71	**eater of beef**	referring to the belief that beef dulled the mind, as in the insult 'beef-witted' in *Troilus and Cressida* (II.1.13)
78	**tongues**	pronounced in the same way as curling 'tongs', hence the following **pun** on hair styling
94	**kickshawses**	trifles, worthless knick-knacks
96	**betters**	social superiors
	old man	experienced person, but perhaps with a reference to Sir Toby's age
97	**galliard**	a lively dance-step
98	**caper**	pun on 'dance' and 'spice' for cooking mutton
100	**back-trick**	innuendo, referring to reverse steps in the dance but with sexual connotations perhaps following on from 'mutton', slang term for a prostitute
105	**coranto**	a fast dance
106	**sink-apace**	an anglicised version of the French 'cinquepas', a dance like a galliard
109	**dun-coloured stock**	brown stockings
111	**Taurus**	astrological signs were thought to govern particular parts of the body

CONTEXT **A04**

At lines 103–4 there is a reference to 'Mistress Mall's picture': pictures were often protected by curtains, though this may be a specific reference to a contemporary scandal about one of Elizabeth I's maids of honour, Mary Fitton, who was disgraced after giving birth to the Earl of Pembroke's illegitimate child in 1601.

ACT I SCENE 4

SUMMARY

- The discussion between Valentine and Viola, dressed in male clothing as Cesario, indicates that Viola is already in Orsino's confidence.
- The Duke's quick intimacy with his new attendant is immediately evident when Orsino arrives, as he dismisses his other servants to be alone with Cesario.
- Orsino notices Cesario's feminine looks.
- Orsino then despatches Viola/Cesario to Olivia to woo her in his place, promising great fortune if she succeeds.
- Viola's final aside reveals that she is herself in love with Orsino.

ANALYSIS

ORSINO AND CESARIO

In this scene the main plot moves forward and develops in complexity, establishing the basis of the comic mistakes and confusion to come. In her disguise as Cesario, Viola seems to combine the physical qualities of both male and female (see **Part Three: Themes**, on **Gender**). Orsino has been able to confide in his new servant, and has clearly formed a trusting attachment to Cesario. The companionship on which their ultimate marriage will be founded is thus immediately established, and by choosing not to show us the early scenes of this relationship, Shakespeare presents it to us as quickly, but solidly begun.

STUDY FOCUS: IRONY   A02

This scene turns on the **dramatic irony** arising from the difference in knowledge between the audience and the characters of Illyria. Valentine's opening words 'you are no stranger' (line 3) while true in one sense are ironic since Viola is indeed a stranger to them all. Orsino says 'Thou know'st no less but all' (line 12), unaware that Viola knows more than he realises. His speech on Cesario's femininity (lines 30–5) gets ironically close to the truth and also establishes the gender confusion which is to become increasingly important to the plot's comic complications (see **Part Three: Themes**, on **Gender**). There's irony, too, in Orsino's promise of shared fortunes if Viola is successful in gaining Olivia for him. Sharing in Orsino's life, in his fortunes both material and circumstantial, is exactly what Viola is aiming at, but through marrying Orsino herself rather than securing him another wife. As the play continues, look out for the way the dramatic irony arising from Viola's disguise continues to work.

KEY QUOTATION: ACT I SCENE 4   A01

In an aside, Viola says: 'Yet a barful strife!/ Whoe'er I woo, myself would be his wife.' (lines 40–1)

- Having just agreed to Orsino's request to woo Olivia on his behalf, Viola, with characteristic clarity and directness, secretly confesses her love for him.
- The **rhyming couplet** ends the scene, ensuring the information divulged to the audience has maximum dramatic impact.
- Part of the humour for the audience now derives from our double advantage over Orsino, since we know not only that Cesario is a woman but also that the 'boy' wants to marry him.

GRADE BOOSTER   A01

Orsino's simple admission of his intimacy with Viola/ Cesario in lines 12–13 is in sharp contrast to the elevated diction of his professions of love for Olivia in the first scene. Trace some differences in Orsino's language between the two scenes. What do they suggest about his relationship with Cesario as compared with Olivia?

GLOSSARY

4   **his humour** his changeability

11 **aloof** apart

12 **unclasped** ornate books were often fastened together with clasps

14 **address thy gait** direct your steps

27 **nuncio** messenger
    aspect appearance

31 **rubious** ruby-red
    pipe voice

33 **semblative** resembles
    part role (referring to the fact that women's roles were taken by male actors)

34 **constellation** character as decided by the stars

40 **barful strife** inner struggle

ACT I SCENE 5

SUMMARY

- Set in Olivia's household, this scene introduces the characters of Olivia herself, her steward Malvolio and the clown Feste.
- Feste tries to jest Olivia out of her melancholy and Malvolio expresses his disapproval of the clown.
- Viola arrives on Orsino's behalf, and is granted an audience with Olivia.
- During their private conversation in which Viola tells her of Orsino's love, it seems that Olivia is falling in love with the messenger (whom she believes to be a young man).
- Olivia sends Malvolio after Viola to give her a ring and with the message for her to return the next day to hear the 'reasons' why Olivia cannot accept Orsino.

ANALYSIS

GRADE BOOSTER **A02**

Shakespeare's fools don't just provide comic business; their foolery, jokes, riddles and songs tell truths and remind us of what it is to be human. As Feste says, 'I wear not motley in my brain' (I.5.46). Professor Jonathan Bate, in *The Genius of Shakespeare* (1997), has called Shakespeare's use of fooling not his philosophy, but his 'foolosophy'. Explore how Feste uses his foolish wisdom in this scene to prove that those around him are also fools.

OLIVIA: A COUNTESS IN MOURNING?

Olivia has been mentioned in each of the three preceding scenes, building audience expectations: now we see her for the first time, and the impression does not entirely accord with the accounts we have been given of her. Rather than being a 'cloistress' (I.1.28), she seems a capable head of her household, engaging in wordplay with her fool, delivering her opinion of Malvolio and of her kinsman Sir Toby, and apparently enjoying her interview with Viola. The scene is characterised throughout by a back-and-forth kind of conversation which speaks of informal social relations. At Olivia's entrance, she maintains the relaxed **rhythms** of prose which began the scene: she clearly does not

stand on ceremony in contrast to Valentine's image of her trapped by her ritual of mourning (I.1). She enjoys an easygoing relationship with Feste, and speaks lightly, perhaps jokingly, to Malvolio. Some productions use the contrast between the view of Olivia from Orsino's household with what we see in this scene to suggest that in fact her mourning has been a smokescreen to deter Orsino's unwelcome advances; others, to suggest a more complicated picture than the goddess of Orsino's desires.

MALVOLIO: A KILLJOY

The introduction of Malvolio (whose name, Mal – ill, volio – will, suggests 'malevolence') is stark and dramatic. He has been a silent and enigmatic presence in the exchange between Feste and Olivia. (Shakespeare uses a similar technique in Act I Scene 2 of *Hamlet* when the prince, in mourning, remains silent and brooding for much of the scene and then utters his cryptic first line.) Malvolio's opening words in response to Olivia's question about Feste, 'Doth he not mend?' (line 60), are brutal and cutting and identify the steward as a killjoy: 'Yes, and shall do, till the pangs of death shake him; infirmity that decays the wise, doth ever make the better fool' (lines 61–2). Unlike his mistress, he is disdainful of Feste's wit and wonders why Olivia

'takes delight in such a barren rascal' (line 67). Olivia's analysis of Malvolio as being 'sick of self-love' (line 73) is an early indication of how the plot will unfold, but it can be related to Viola's shrewd observation of Olivia herself later in the scene: 'You are too proud' (line 205). Malvolio is the most extreme version of a type we keep encountering in the play, as a kind of narcissism preoccupies many of its main protagonists. Olivia's subsequent rebuke of him, however, as lacking generosity and a 'free disposition' (lines 74–5) points to a key difference in him which will ultimately leave him isolated.

STUDY FOCUS: PLAYING A PART   A02

In her audience with Olivia, Viola uses the **imagery** of theatre simultaneously to advance and to undermine her message of Orsino's love. She talks of her 'part' (line 149), admits that 'I am not that I play' (line 153), and mentions the speech she must deliver as if it were a script she has learned: 'I took great pains to study it, and 'tis poetical' (line 160). The developing intimacy between the two is revealed as Olivia echoes this imagery: 'You are now out of your text' (line 190), i.e. you are going beyond your scripted lines. She takes up the task of deflating high-blown love **rhetoric**, reducing the conventional poetic device known as the **blazon**, in which the lover's eyes, lips, cheeks and hair are separately discussed in **clichéd** terms, to a **bathetic** catalogue: 'as, *item*, two lips, indifferent red; *item*, two grey eyes, with lids to them' (lines 202–3). All of the main characters in *Twelfth Night* take on masks, assume postures and perform roles, and the theatre imagery is not simply a reference to Viola's disguise, but is a teasing reminder of the fact that we are watching a play and so we too are implicated in the playing of roles. Find some more references to theatre in the play and examples of characters adopting roles.

CONTEXT   A04

The Royal Shakespeare Company production of the play directed by Peter Gill in 1974 used the set to embody the idea of self-love by having the stage dominated by a huge mural of the classical Narcissus, who fell in love with his own reflection and so became a prototype of the self-obsessed individual (see **Part Three: Themes**, on **Love and self-love**).

CHECK THE FILM   A03

Trevor Nunn's 1996 film made it clear, through showing Feste's implacable stare at Malvolio, that this scene **foreshadows** the hostility between the two which will have its open expression in Act IV Scene 2.

VIOLA AND OLIVIA

In her first encounter with Olivia, Viola comically alternates between an apparently prepared **eulogy** – 'Most radiant, exquisite, and unmatchable beauty' (line 141) – and the deflating commentary of 'I would be loath to cast away my speech' (lines 142–3) as if she is not addressing it to the right woman. She is not quite disrespectful with Olivia, but almost. Something of this unpompous, rather maverick treatment seems to be what attracts Olivia to Viola. It can be seen that the energy and spontaneity of Viola's witty remarks are much more charismatic than the rather flowery and impersonal language of Orsino's passions in Act I Scene 1, and it is presumably these which prompt Olivia to grant the unprecedented private meeting with this attractive young messenger.

Viola's speech is extremely persuasive: 'Make me a willow cabin at your gate' (line 223) is a powerful invocation to love which, in its intensity, turns up the erotic heat of the encounter. It seems almost a proclamation of love, not by a messenger as a surrogate but by an ardent lover in person, and Olivia responds in kind with her sudden question about parentage, designed to establish the suitability of this potential husband. Throughout the scene, Viola uses the first person 'I' rather than the third person 'he' as a messenger might use ('he told me to tell you that he loves you', for example). The increasingly intense relationship between them could be seen to cut out Orsino, though **ironically** the power of Viola's speech of yearning could derive from her longing for him. It's important to consider how Shakespeare uses the Cesario disguise to play with varieties of sexual desire in Viola's relationships with Olivia and Orsino.

STUDY FOCUS: OLIVIA'S SOLILOQUY   A02

Olivia invites Viola to return, but only to hear more of why she cannot love Orsino, and wishes, in her **soliloquy**, that 'the master were the man' (line 249). She expresses uncertainty about what is happening to her, fearing to find 'Mine eye too great a flatterer for my mind' (line 264) – perhaps she has fallen in love with the looks of this attractive page, rather than made a rational decision about where to bestow her affections. Ultimately, however, in her final soliloquy, she is resigned to see how events unfold, giving – or leaving – control in the hands of fate: 'What is decreed must be; and be this so' (line 266). Compare Olivia's reaction here to Viola's couplet in Act I Scene 2 (lines 60–1) and Viola's response only moments after her encounter with Olivia on discovering that the Countess has fallen in love with her (II.2.37–8). How do these quotations link with the theme of 'chance'?

KEY QUOTATION: ACT I SCENE 5   A01

Olivia: 'Even so quickly may one catch the plague?' (line 250)

- Olivia recognises that she has fallen for Viola/Cesario and likens her feeling to a sickness.
- This **metaphor** continues the references to sickness which appear from the first scene and often in connection with Olivia, for example 'sicken and so die' (I.1.3), 'she purged the air of pestilence' (I.1.20) and 'What a plague means my niece' (I.3.1).
- The **image** is a brief reminder of the darker side of the play's festive, holiday world.
- Her thought is expressed as a question in a soliloquy, which suggests that her feeling of losing control is genuine.

GLOSSARY

5	**fear no colours**	Feste **puns** on 'colours' (military standards) and 'collars' (nooses)
6	**Make that good**	explain
8	**good lenten answer**	a weak joke
17	**let summer bear it**	let the good weather continue, or make it bearable
19	**points**	issues, but Maria puns on the sense of laces holding up breeches
21	**gaskins**	wide breeches
23	**Eve's flesh**	woman
26	**you were best**	it would be best for you
29	**Quinapalus**	apparently, a made-up 'authority': Feste is mocking scholarly pretensions
33	**Go to**	expression of impatience
35	**madonna**	Italian for 'my lady', with definite Catholic associations
38	**botcher**	cobbler
45	**Misprision**	wrongful arrest, and misunderstanding
45–6	*cucullus … monachum*	Latin proverb meaning 'the cowl does not make the monk'
46	**motley**	the multi-coloured garments traditionally worn by fools and jesters
49	**Dexteriously**	dextrously, cleverly
51	**catechise**	question, as in religious litany
53	**idleness**	recreation, amusement
69	**out of his guard**	term from fencing, meaning he has no defence
70	**minister occasion**	provide an opportunity
71	**set**	fixed, not spontaneous
72	**zanies**	professional fools
75	**bird-bolts**	blunt arrows for shooting birds
76	**allowed**	licensed
79	**Mercury**	god of, among other things, deception
84	**well attended**	with several attendants
95	*pia mater*	brain
99–100	**pickle-herring**	presumably, these have induced Sir Toby's eponymous belch
100	**sot**	fool, drunkard
108–9	**above heat**	above the quantity to warm him
111	**crowner**	coroner
	sit	hold an inquest
123	**sheriff's post**	post set up outside a sheriff or mayor's house, denoting his authority
129	**personage**	appearance
131	**squash**	unripe peascod
	peascod	peapod
	codling	unripe apple
132	**standing water**	at the turn of the tide
133	**well-favoured**	handsome
144	**con**	learn by heart
145	**sustain**	suffer
145–6	**comptible … usage**	I am sensitive to the slightest snub
149	**modest**	enough
151	**comedian**	actor
164	**'Tis not … me**	the phases of the moon were associated with lunacy (hence the name)
165	**skipping**	inconsequential
167	**swabber**	deckhand
	hull	anchor
168	**giant**	presumably a joking allusion to Maria's height

GLOSSARY continued

171	**courtesy**	preamble
273	**taxation of homage**	demand for payments to a superior noble
174	**matter**	meaning, significance
177	**entertainment**	reception
180	**text**	theme, as for a sermon
182	**comfortable**	comforting
190	**curtain**	i.e. Olivia's veil
193	**if God did all**	if the beauty is natural, not cosmetic
194	**grain**	colourfast
199	**copy**	child, but Olivia takes it to mean 'record'
202	**labelled to my will**	added to my will
	indifferent	quite, fairly
208	**nonpareil**	unequalled
210	**fertile**	copious
215	**voices well divulged**	well spoken of
	free	generous, well-bred
223	**willow**	associated with unrequited love
225	**cantons**	songs
227	**Hallow**	shout, and bless
228	**babbling gossip**	personification of the echo
233	**state**	estate, standing
239	**fee'd post**	messenger waiting for a tip
248	**blazon**	coat of arms
256	**county**	count
258	**flatter with**	encourage
365	**owe**	own, control

CONTEXT A04

One of Shakespeare's most famous references to theatre in his plays is the speech 'All the world's a stage…' by Jacques in *As You Like It* (Act II Scene 7). This idea of men and women as 'players' on stage suggests that assuming a role involves more than adopting a superficial disguise, and is integral to our human 'being'. Find more examples of Shakespeare referring to theatre and acting in *Twelfth Night*. What effect do they have on the way the audience experiences the drama?

EXTENDED COMMENTARY

ACT I SCENE 5 LINES 139–207

This first encounter between Viola and Olivia establishes the flirtatious, mocking tone of their relationship. Viola enters and does not know, or affects not to know (it depends on how the scene is staged), which one of the women is Olivia. Launching into a prepared speech of compliments with a poetic **apostrophe** – 'Most radiant, exquisite, and unmatchable beauty' (line 141) – Viola breaks off anticlimactically to check that this is indeed her intended audience. This prose interjection into her own speech deflates Orsino's romantic pretensions, and the repeated references to the speech's artificiality as 'excellently well penned, I have taken great pains to con it' (lines 143–4), 'I took great pains to study it and 'tis poetical' (line 160) serve to undermine the message. Viola's ambivalence towards her role as surrogate wooer for the man she herself loves seems to find voice in this **ironic** undercutting of her master's words. The real irony of the situation, however, is that it is in her own voice that she is most attractive to Olivia.

Immediately, it is the messenger rather than the message that attracts Olivia. Her first response is to ask a question: 'Whence came you, sir?' (line 147). Viola turns this to her purpose by stressing that it is outside her 'part' (line 149), and a run of **images** drawn from acting and the theatre includes Olivia's question 'Are you a comedian?' (line 151). Viola seems to be enjoying the disjunction between the role she is playing and her true self, and her hints at this discrepancy have the effect of arousing Olivia's curiosity still further. 'I am not that I play' (line 153) is countered by Olivia's reply 'If I do not usurp myself, I am' (line 154). This curious response may suggest that Olivia, too, recognises a disjunction between the 'I' and the 'lady of the house' and that she sees her own dividedness echoed in this mysterious young messenger. There are many similarities between Viola and Olivia, not made explicit in the scene, and it may be that their evident shared enjoyment in their conversation derives from their implicit awareness of this.

Throughout the scene, Viola dominates. She tends to begin verbal tricks that Olivia then picks up and returns, such as the religious connotations of 'divinity' and 'profanation' (line 178), prompting Olivia's echoing 'divinity' and 'text' (lines 179–80). It is as if their conversation is a kind of tennis match where each player is learning the style and movement of the other. They speak in prose, suggesting a relaxed kind of intimacy, and this is stressed when Olivia dismisses Maria and her attendants. Alone with Olivia for the first time, Viola has another attempt at her set speech, but by now the ostensible reason for her audience has been overtaken, and Olivia is quickly dismissive, interrupting for the first time at line 183. The shorter to-and-fro speeches of lines 184–94 are, to continue the image of the tennis match, a quick rally which gets the heart racing, and there is an element of eroticism in Viola's invitation to Olivia to unveil herself. It's not clear why Viola should ask this, but her love for Orsino might explain her need to see the object of his desire.

Viola's feeling of intimacy with Olivia leads her to continue their joking. She speaks to her as an equal, not in the reverential tones of an underling, and perhaps it is this freshness that so attracts Olivia. Elsewhere Orsino and Malvolio independently observe that the figure of Cesario is not unambiguously masculine: this, too, is part of the messenger's attraction for Olivia. Viola's tone is more akin to Feste's than to the laboured **clichés** of her would-be lover Orsino. Olivia's mock inventory of her looks may suggest an almost skittish, girlish joking, or it may be a more brittle self-mockery. This is a vulnerable person, hiding, perhaps, behind mourning and its physical **symbol**, the veil, here newly revealed. Her strange visitor is quick to characterise her, and not entirely flatteringly, describing Olivia as 'too proud', but with an apparently sincere tone, 'if you were the devil, you are fair' (lines 205–6). The 'text' has been left far behind, and this unscripted exchange adds fuel to the fire in an already tense situation. There is a palpable energy in the conversation between the two women, as Viola finds herself the go-between and third party in an erotic triangle.

CONTEXT **A04**

On the Elizabethan stage women were played by boy actors. The convention adds a further level of complexity to the performance of this scene which becomes one between two boys, profoundly affecting the erotic interplay between the actors and hence the audience reaction; Viola is a boy acting as a woman dressed as a boy and Olivia is a boy acting as a woman. As a result, the part of Olivia now becomes central in this performance of gender. It was the role that actor Mark Rylance played In the 'original practice' all-male production at Shakespeare's Globe Theatre (2002, revived 2012).

ACT II SCENE 1

SUMMARY

- Antonio has saved Sebastian, Viola's twin brother, from drowning in the shipwreck.
- Sebastian, who has been calling himself Roderigo, is in mourning for Viola, and tells Antonio his real name.
- Antonio wants to be his servant, but Sebastian decides to go to Orsino's court.
- Antonio is in a hostile country where he has many enemies, but will not leave Sebastian because of his love for him.

GRADE BOOSTER · A02

In his earlier play *The Comedy of Errors*, Shakespeare uses the device of identical twins, in that case two sets, to create comic confusion and farcical situations arising from mistaken identity. In *Twelfth Night*, the device is used in a more profound way to disturb the idea of a single, fixed identity and so question the nature of identity itself. Trace how other characters in the play react to the doubling effect they experience when encountering Viola/Cesario and Sebastian.

ANALYSIS

A TWIN APPEARS

The last act ended with Olivia giving up her situation to fate, inviting this mysterious power to 'show thy force' (I.5.265). Sebastian's immediate introduction, therefore, is a direct indication that this power is to be benevolent. In place of the woman Olivia is in love with, a male version, similar in appearance – 'it was said she much resembled me' (line 18) – is introduced. The **imagery** of fate is immediately echoed by Sebastian – 'My stars shine

darkly over me' (line 2) – and so even before they meet, the pair are linked by a shared vocabulary to explain events. Similarly, the soon-to-be-lovers are connected by their association with weeping: Sebastian's 'salt water' remembrance of his dead sister (line 22) links with the 'eye-offending brine' of Olivia's tears for her brother (I.1.30). In contrast to Viola's reaction in Act I Scene 2, Sebastian is in a cheerless mood and he seems close to 'unmanly' tears: 'I am yet so near the manners of my mother that … mine eyes will tell tales of me' (lines 29–31). The effect of his gloomy language – 'malignancy', 'distemper', 'evils', 'bad recompense' (lines 3–5) – is tempered, however, by our superior knowledge. We know that Viola is not in fact drowned, and any suspicion that nor was Sebastian is now confirmed.

BONDS AND BARRIERS

The parameters of what can, and cannot, happen in the play are thus carefully established, and the grief which has characterised both twins is registered as mistaken. The firm expectation is of eventual reunion. The scene adds to our knowledge of Viola's situation too: the force of each sibling's feeling of bereavement is strengthened with the information that they are twins, and parallels between Viola and Olivia are further developed with the news that Viola's father, too, has died (line 13). In romantic comedy parents are often a barrier to love, but in this play, without parents to create the obstacles, the barriers lie within the characters themselves.

STUDY FOCUS: TRUE DEVOTION A02

Antonio's strong feelings for the younger Sebastian are expressed here in a structural parallel with the preceding scene, where Olivia declares her love in a short **soliloquy** (I.5.250–4), perhaps to **foreshadow** the fact that Olivia and Antonio will, in a sense, be rivals for Sebastian's affections. In a soliloquy Antonio declares that he will not abandon his friend. Like Viola and Olivia before him, he is prepared to risk himself: 'come what may' and his words are unexpectedly intense, even passionate, 'I do adore thee so/ That danger shall seem sport' (lines 35–6). The fact that it is delivered as verse, as opposed to the prose of the rest of the scene, gives it importance and its speaker a particular status: he is not a 'servant' (line 26) as Maria is to Olivia. Many productions have made sense of this by suggesting that Antonio has sexual feelings for Sebastian (see **Part Three: Characters** and **Part Five: Critical Debates**). Examine Antonio's words in this scene. How does Shakespeare quickly convey the force of Antonio's devotion?

KEY QUOTATION: ACT II SCENE 1 A02

Sebastian: '…both born in an hour'. (lines 13–14)

- Sebastian reveals that he and Viola are not only brother and sister, but twins.
- They closely resemble one another, which immediately promises a resolution to the problem of Olivia's love for Viola which arose in the previous scene.

- With this detail, Shakespeare now provides the audience with more information than any of the characters, including Viola, allowing for the development of even greater comic confusion and **dramatic irony**.

CONTEXT A04

William Shakespeare was the father of twins. They were christened Hamnet and Judith in Holy Trinity Church, Stratford-upon-Avon on 2 February 1585. Exactly seventeen years later *Twelfth Night* was performed in Middle Temple, London, but Judith was now without her twin brother who had died five-and-half-years before on 4 August 1596. Although it is not possible to confirm biographical links to *Twelfth Night*, it is perhaps significant that in this play Shakespeare sets the union of romantic lovers within the broader frame of the restoration of a lost brother to his twin sister.

GLOSSARY

1	**Nor will you not**	do you not want me to
2	**darkly**	unfavourably
3	**malignancy**	bad luck, evil influence (derived from astrology)
	distemper	disorder, disturb
7	**determinate**	planned
	extravagancy	wandering
12	**Messaline**	a Shakespearean piece of geography, which may refer to modern-day Marseilles
16	**breach**	surf, breaking waves
20	**estimable**	appreciative
21	**publish**	speak openly of
24	**entertainment**	hospitality
26	**murder me**	cause me to die (through being parted from you)
29	**kindness**	tenderness
29–30	**manners of my mother**	Sebastian means that he is close to weeping (seen as a womanish characteristic)
32	**gentleness**	favour

GLOSSARY

1   **even** just

2–3 **but hither** only this far

6   **desperate assurance** certainty that it is hopeless

7   **hardy** foolhardy, bold

13   **in your eye** where you can see it

17   **lost** made her lose

25   **pregnant enemy** ever watchful enemy (i.e. the devil)

26   **proper-false** attractive but deceitful men

27   **set their forms** the **image** is of women's hearts like molten wax being impressed by men

29   **such as we … we be** since we are made of frail flesh, we are frail

30   **fadge** turn out

31   **monster** i.e. both man and woman

36   **thriftless** wasted

ACT II SCENE 2

SUMMARY

- Malvolio is sent by Olivia to give Viola a ring.
- Viola tries to refuse the gift by pretending that she gave it to Olivia.
- Malvolio throws it down to her before stalking off.
- Viola realises that Olivia has fallen in love with her as Cesario.
- Viola leaves it to time to unravel the tangled situation.

ANALYSIS

'TOO HARD A KNOT …'?

The prose exchange between Malvolio and Viola confirms Malvolio's bad-tempered character. The scene is, however, most significant in giving us Viola's only **soliloquy** in the play, in which she realises that her 'outside' has 'charmed' Olivia (line 15) and concludes 'I am the man' (line 22). Viola responds by making some general comments about women in love, where she is talking as much about her own plight, helplessly in love with Orsino, as she is about Olivia, and so again draws a parallel between their situations. She summarises the action so far and cannot see how this complicated situation – where she, as a woman, loves her master, who loves Olivia, who loves her, thinking she is a man – is going to be resolved, and feels pity for the 'poor lady' (line 23). Ultimately, it must be settled by the passage of time: 'O time, thou must untangle this, not I;/ It is too hard a knot for me t'untie' (lines 37–8). The audience, however, can see a resolution because we know that Sebastian, her lookalike twin brother, is 'the man' and he is alive.

STUDY FOCUS: VIOLA'S SOLILOQUY   **A02**

Viola's mind is racing as she works out that Olivia loves her, explains why and speculates on the consequences. Her speech contains a series of questions some of which are direct, 'what means this lady?' (line 14), and some **rhetorical**, 'What thriftless sighs shall poor Olivia breathe?' (line 36). She **apostrophises** her disguise as 'a wickedness' (line 24) which has the power to shape women's 'waxen hearts' (line 28) with a false impression due to 'our frailty' (line 27). Her interrupted **syntax**, 'indeed so much/ That, methought' (lines 16–17), 'if it be so, as 'tis'(line 22), and her exclamations, 'Fortune forbid…' (line 15), 'Alas' (line 28), attest to the emotional and psychological disruption caused by this complicated situation. However, perhaps the regularity of the **rhyming couplet** which concludes the scene (lines 37–8) reassures us that all will indeed be well. Analyse in detail Viola's speech by finding more examples of questions, disrupted syntax, exclamations and rhyming to show how the form of the words creates a vivid sense of her thought process. How does her soliloquy affect her relationship with the audience?

ACT II SCENE 3

SUMMARY

- Sir Andrew Aguecheek and Sir Toby Belch make merry late in the evening, accompanied by Feste's songs.
- Maria warns them about the noise they are making and that they are in danger of being turned out of the house.
- Their revelry is interrupted by a furious Malvolio, but they ignore him.
- Malvolio implicates Maria in the rowdiness and threatens to tell Olivia.
- Maria eagerly takes on the task of repaying Malvolio and hatches a plot to humiliate him by forging a letter pretending Olivia is in love with him.
- Sir Toby and Sir Andrew agree the plan and Maria leaves, encouraging them to go to bed.
- Sir Toby tells Sir Andrew to send for more money and finally decides that it is too late to go to bed.

ANALYSIS

RESTRAINT AND EXCESS

The antipathy between Malvolio and the rowdy house-guests might have been anticipated from what we have learnt of each party so far, but here they are brought into open conflict. Malvolio's entrance sees him turn his contempt on the knights, in a combination of deference and insult: 'My masters, are you mad?' (line 75). He summons the authority of the Countess Olivia to issue demands – 'separate yourself and your misdemeanours' – and threats, 'she is very willing to bid you farewell' (lines 83–5). His interruption of the festivities draws up the battle lines: between the hedonistic philosophy of Sir Toby and Sir Andrew's view of life (lines 9–12) and the 'puritan' austerity of Malvolio's behaviour. While he has a professional responsibility, as steward, to exercise a prudent eye on the household economy, Sir Andrew and Sir Toby are devoted to eating and drinking. It is a clash between restraint and excess, between carefulness and extravagance. No wonder that the audience is usually on the side of the revellers, rather than the 'party-pooper'.

CONTEXT **A04**

A late medieval Dutch painting by Pieter Brueghel characterises a similar clash between temperance and immoderation in **allegorical** terms. In 'The Fight between Carnival and Lent' (1559) a figure in the red and yellow colours of the jester leads another in a sombre habit through a sixteenth-century festival.

CHECK THE PLAY **A03**

Maria warns Sir Toby and the revellers, 'If my lady have not called up her steward Malvolio and bid him turn you out of doors, never trust me' (lines 63–5). In *King Lear*, we see a tragic enactment of what Sir Toby and the revellers are threatened with here. In response to the riotous behaviour of Lear with his knights, Regan's words to Gloucester, repeated by Cornwall, 'Shut up your doors' (II.4.299– 303), mean that Lear is cast out on the heath in a storm.

TIME

The scene mixes rollicking low comedy and sad reflection to create a distinctive blend of light and dark elements which becomes an increasing feature of the play's mood. There is also an edge of irritation amid the jesting in the exchanges between Sir Andrew and Feste: 'I shall be constrain'd in't to call thee knave, knight' (lines 57–8). Feste's song, as in the Epilogue, contributes to the sense of melancholy permeating the play and this is true too of the scene's numerous references to time. Sir Toby classes being up after midnight as a form of early rising – being 'up betimes' (line 2) – whereas Sir Andrew, more prosaically, asserts that 'to be up late is to be up late' (lines 3–4). But in the idea of 'What's to come is still unsure … Youth's a stuff will not endure' (lines 43–6), these hours take on a significance of people trying to beat the clock, live a short life to the full (see **Part Three: Themes**, on **Excess**). Malvolio, 'a time-pleaser' (line 125), seems to steward hours and minutes as well as drink and money, in contrast to Sir Toby's extravagant spending on all counts. Feste's song stands as a comment on the action of the play so far – in an analogy to Olivia's speech (at I.5.265–6) and Viola's 'time, thou must untangle this, not I' (II.2.37) – and thus serves a **choric** role (see **Part Two: Characterisation**). It is interesting to note the way Feste's songs here and at the end of the play adopt different perspectives on the passage of time.

STUDY FOCUS: THE FEISTY MARIA [A01]

Here the major subplot, the tricking of Malvolio, led by the feisty Maria, is established. She takes control of the plot of 'revenge' (line 129), having been least directly insulted by Malvolio, but patronised as 'Mistress Mary' (line 103) and indirectly threatened by him, 'she shall know of it, by this hand' (line 105). She has a clear-sighted and merciless view of her victim's weakness, and is described as an Amazon queen, 'Penthesilea' (line 149), in reference to the legendary race of strong women. Perhaps this praise is an early indication of Sir Toby's admiration for her. She perceives that Malvolio believes that 'all that look on him love him' (line 128) – an echo of Olivia's earlier charge of 'self-love' (I.5.73) – and thus the trap is set. Maria's list in her mock-praise of his appearance uses the same **blazon** device – 'the colour of his beard, the shape of his leg, the manner of his gait, the expressure of his eye, forehead and complexion' (lines 132–3) – as Olivia in her praise of Cesario – 'Thy tongue, thy face, thy limbs, actions, and spirit/ Do give thee fivefold blazon' (I.5.247–8) – thus developing the play's mocking stance towards love conventions and literary **clichés** (see **Part Three: Themes**, on **Love and self-love**). Having begun by warning the revellers about Malvolio, why does Maria take charge of the plot against him?

KEY QUOTATION: ACT II SCENE 3 [A01]

Sir Toby: 'Dost thou think because thou art virtuous there shall be no more cakes and ale?' (lines 97–9)

● Sir Toby challenges Malvolio's right to impose his puritanical codes of behaviour on the revellers.

● In one inebriated, but eloquent **rhetorical** question, Sir Toby dismisses sobriety – both literally and in the wider **metaphorical** sense of the attempt to deny appetite and pleasure.

● Feste defiantly aligns himself with Sir Toby with a similar undeniable truth of the body: 'Yes, by St Anne, and ginger shall be hot i'th'mouth too' (line 100).

● This clash between revelry and repression establishes the conflict which will lead to Malvolio's inevitable undoing.

● The distinctive mixture of humour and melancholy in *Twelfth Night* partly arises from the fact that the spirit of revelry is expressed in the face of threats against it, as money, time and tolerance are all running out.

GLOSSARY

2	**betimes**	early

diluculo surgere part of a Latin proverb, well known from an Elizabethan school textbook. The full proverb 'diluculo surgere saluberrimum est' means 'to get up at dawn is most healthy'

5	**can**	tankard
8	**four elements**	i.e. air, earth, fire and water
12	**stoup**	tankard holding two pints or one litre
14–15	**We Three**	referring to the caption on popular pictures showing two fools' or asses' heads – the third was the viewer
17	**breast**	lungs for singing
20–1	**Pigrogromitus … Vapians … Queubus**	probably Sir Toby's imitation of Feste's mock learning
22	**leman**	sweetheart
23	**impeticos**	pocket (a **nonce word**)

gratillity gratuity (again, a nonce word)

24	**Myrmidons**	in Greek myth, the race of people led by Achilles. Feste's speech is **bathetic** in stating these obvious absurdities

bottle-ale apparently used to denote inferior ale, hence low-grade taverns

29	**testril**	sixpence piece
30–2	**good life**	the joke is on different meanings: either a drinking song, or a moral song or hymn
38	**Every wise man's son**	proverbially, wise men were supposed to have foolish sons
51	**welkin**	sky
52	**souls**	music was thought to draw the soul out of the body
54	**dog at**	good at
66	**Cataian**	Chinese – meaning that Olivia is inscrutable
67	**Peg-a-Ramsey**	referring to a ballad about a spying wife, so suggesting that Malvolio is on the lookout
68	**consanguineous**	closely related (as Sir Toby goes on to explain)

Tilly vally nonsense

70	**Beshrew me**	curse me
78	**coziers**	cobblers
78–9	**mitigation or remorse of voice**	lowering your voices or consideration
80	**Sneck up**	roughly equivalent to 'Get lost'
81	**round**	blunt
82–3	**nothing allied**	no relation
101	**rub your chain with crumbs**	a way of cleaning metal; referring to Malvolio's badge of office
104	**uncivil rule**	disorderly behaviour
108	**the field**	i.e. to a duel
114	**gull**	trick
115	**ayword**	proverb
118	**Possess us**	tell us (put us in possession of your thoughts)
125	**time-pleaser**	time-server

cons state without book learns elevated language by heart

134	**feelingly personated**	appropriately described
136	**hands**	handwritings
155	**recover**	win
157	**cut**	a term of abuse, perhaps referring to a gelding
159	**burn some sack**	warm and spice some sack, a white wine from Spain

GRADE BOOSTER **AO2**

Don't ignore seemingly simple lines. Think about the ways you could interpret Sir Andrew's 'I care not for a good life' (II.3.32). Does this show his ignorant misunderstanding of the phrase, 'a good life' (thinking it means a virtuous life), or is he clever enough to deliberately **pun** on the idea of having fun?

ACT II SCENE 4

SUMMARY

- Orsino is with his attendants, and Feste is sent for in order to play an old song which Orsino requests.
- Viola's appreciation of the music leads Orsino to ask her if she is in love.
- Feste plays the melancholy song which tells of a man who longs for death because of his unrequited love.
- Orsino is spurred on again to seek Olivia's love, saying that no woman could love as strongly as he does.
- Viola contradicts him by telling a story about her 'sister' (really herself), who was deeply in love but unable to tell of her feelings.
- Orsino is moved to ask whether the 'sister' died of her love, to which Viola gives an enigmatic response.
- Viola reminds Orsino about Olivia and she is sent off to her with another jewel as a love token from Orsino.

CHECK THE PLAY   **AO3**

In Shakespeare's earlier play featuring a heroine who dresses as a man, *As You Like It*, Rosalind, in contrast to Viola, appears as herself in women's clothing when she first meets Orlando, and has companionship throughout her masquerade from her cousin Celia who knows about her disguise. How do these differences alter the dramatic effect of the male disguises in each play?

ANALYSIS

YEARNING

This vital scene (discussed in more detail in the **Extended Commentary: Act II Scene 4 lines 83–120**) establishes the power of Viola's feelings for Orsino and his deepening attachment to her. She has two chances to talk about her love for him, once when she mentions her love of someone who bears a strong resemblance to him, and then when she uses the alias of her 'sister' trapped in an unexpressed love. Her disguise has made her utterly alone, since she cannot be herself to anyone. The **image** of the sister pining away for love is one of forlorn recognition, since Viola is in a situation without an obvious (to her) hope of resolution. The sadness underlining the scene is made explicit when the talk of siblings reminds Viola of the loss of her brother.

IDEAS OF LOVE

Another aspect of the scene is how the couple get an unprecedented chance to discuss their ideas about love. Given how regimented conventional aristocratic courtships were in the Elizabethan period, it would have been highly unlikely that, in her women's clothes, Viola could spend time alone with Orsino if they were not married. One consequence of her disguise is that she is able to gain a kind of intimacy with Orsino in the guise of a man which, **paradoxically**, would be impossible were she to appear as a woman.

STUDY FOCUS: CHANGES IN ORSINO A01

Orsino's own attitudes seem contradictory. In Act I he praised Olivia for her constancy to the memory of her dead brother, and here he begins by admitting that, indeed, women are more steadfast than men in matters of the heart: 'Our fancies are more giddy and unfirm,/ More longing, wavering, sooner lost and worn,/ Than women's are' (lines 31–3). He then fulfils Feste's comment on him as 'changeable taffeta' (line 71) by contradicting himself and stating that it is men who are better able to bear the strength of the passion of love (lines 89–90), and that women's hearts 'lack retention' (line 92) and can only offer the brief and quickly sated 'appetite' (line 93) in return (see the **Extended Commentary: Act II Scene 4 lines 83–120**). Trace the changes in Orsino's attitudes to love so far in the play. How does this scene demonstrate that a more enduring bond is developing between him and Viola?

REVISION FOCUS: TASK 1 A02

How far do you agree with the following statements?

- The lasting impression left by this scene is of sad reflection rather than comic misunderstanding.
- The impression of Orsino as self-obsessed and self-pitying is increased, not lessened, by what he says to Viola about love.

Try writing opening paragraphs for essays based on these discussion points. Set out your arguments clearly.

CHECK THE FILM A03

Trevor Nunn set this scene around various masculine pursuits such as card-playing, smoking and billiards to portray how the Cesario disguise enables Viola to meet and get to know her beloved on male territory. Kenneth Branagh's production brought out the exquisite tenderness between Orsino and Viola as she speaks of her 'sister' and he becomes increasingly drawn to his servant 'boy'.

GLOSSARY

5	**recollected terms**	studied phrases (fashionable around the time the play was written)
19–20	**very echo … throned**	it reflects the feelings of the heart
22	**stayed upon some favour**	fixed on some face
28	**wears she to him**	adapts herself to him (as clothes to their wearer)
29	**sways she level**	exerts a consistent influence
35	**hold the bent**	remain at full stretch (a **metaphor** from archery)
37	**displayed**	opened
42	**spinsters**	spinners
44	**silly sooth**	simple truth
45	**dallies with**	lingers on
46	**old age**	the good old days, or the golden age of poetry
50	**cypress**	either a coffin of cypress wood, or one decked with cypress branches
70	**melancholy god**	Saturn
71	**changeable taffeta**	shot silk, which changes with the light
76	**sovereign cruelty**	cruel mistress
77	**world**	society
79	**parts**	status, possessions
80	**giddily**	lightly
81	**miracle**	Olivia's beauty
82	**pranks**	adorns
84	**Sooth**	in truth
94	**motion**	impulse
108	**damask**	pink and white, like a damask rose
109	**green and yellow**	the pallor of melancholy
113	**Our shows … will**	we show more than we feel

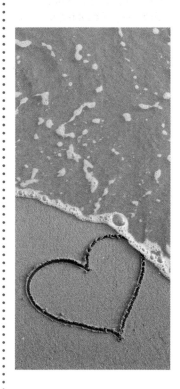

EXTENDED COMMENTARY

CHECK THE PLAY **A03**

Dramatic irony occurs throughout Shakespeare's plays, but it can do more than create tension, humour or mockery. In *The Merchant of Venice*, Portia disguises herself in order to play the part of a male lawyer at a trial in the most important scene of the play, Act IV Scene 1, in which her husband's best friend, Antonio, may meet his death. Her husband, Bassanio, is also present at the trial, unaware of the lawyer's real identity. It is in this scene that Portia's judgement and intelligence are most apparent as she delivers Antonio from his fate, but what does it tell us about the role of women that we see her cleverness through the lens of male disguise?

ACT II SCENE 4 LINES 83–120

Viola's attempts to persuade Orsino that Olivia may not love him employ a kind of reverse psychology: she does not agree with him that women are incapable of 'so strong a passion' (line 90) but rather tries to make him believe that women bear a more constant love than men. She tells him how women's love can be as strong as men's by encouraging him to imagine that a woman loves him as much as he loves Olivia. It is the first of the manoeuvres by which this oblique, yet intimate, conversation progresses. Viola confesses her love for Orsino via imaginary triangulations with this woman who might possibly love him, and through her sister who loved but never articulated it.

Viola suggests that, if she were a woman, she might love Orsino as her sister (or, with even more circumlocution, her father's daughter) loved a man. Interestingly, she seems to dare to broach this only in the context of his rejection of her love: 'You cannot love her./ You tell her so' (lines 87–8). She counters Orsino's easy assumption that passionate love is an exclusively masculine quality with the **image** of the constant, pining woman who 'sat like Patience on a monument,/ Smiling at grief' (lines 110–11). Orsino becomes interested in this tale, but his own masochistic interpretation of true love is displayed in his question, 'But died thy sister of her love' (line 115). Perhaps the

familiar address 'my boy' at the end of this line is the nearest Orsino gets to explicit affection for his page. The word 'love' breathes like a sigh through the lines as both characters nurse a love that cannot be requited. Viola's vacillation between her female self, 'I am all the daughters of my father's house' (line 116), and her male appearance, 'We men' (line 112), comes as close as she dares to revealing herself (see **Part Three: Themes**, on **Gender**). The use of the fake first-person plural 'we' and the equally bogus third-person 'she' shows how desperately Viola is thinking about different identities and the strain of these adjustments during her disguise. Almost her only use of the pronoun 'I' in the scene comes as a conditional: 'were I a woman' (line 104).

The dramatic irony of Orsino's glib sexism, 'man to man' with the woman whom he does not know is in love with him, makes for comedy as well as **pathos** in the scene. Orsino is almost competitive in the extent of his love, with an appetite 'as hungry as the sea' (line 96) in an image which connects him to Viola, spat out by the sea on the shore of Illyria in Act I Scene 2. In contrast to his imagery of love as ravenous eating (see **Part Three: Themes**, on **Love and self-love**), Viola's imaginary sister is eaten up by her unspoken love, 'like a worm i'th'bud' (line 107) – an image of something destroyed before it has the chance even to blossom. The imagery seems to suggest that it is Orsino's love which is active and masculine, and Viola's which is passive and feminine, but in fact neither is true: throughout, Viola has been a kind of catalyst or active agent (see **Part Two: Characterisation**) and, as Act V Scene 1 shows, Orsino reacts rather than instigates.

The account of the 'blank' history of Viola's father's daughter (line 106) is a shadow of how this play of unrequited love could, but will not, turn out. It is one of the ways the comedy flirts, albeit momentarily, with the 'what if' of tragedy. We already know that Sebastian is not drowned, so we know that somehow matters will be resolved. But the scene ends in sadness and an abrupt change of mood. Viola recalls her brother (line 117) and stirs herself to go to Olivia on Orsino's behalf. However, the closeness of this private conversation between Viola and Orsino contrasts with the distant formality of his wooing of Olivia, sending his page with a jewel rather than going in person. This exchange with Viola has established the basis of their ultimate marriage, and we do not see Orsino again, because we do not need to, until the very last scene of the play.

CRITICAL VIEWPOINT **A03**

Characters who 'go missing' from plays, as Orsino does, always invite critical debate. For example, Lady Macbeth is only seen once more in *Macbeth* after Act III Scene 4 – and then as a guilty, and perhaps mad, sleepwalker. Does this represent the silencing of the female voice or is it more a comment on the extent to which Macbeth dominates the second half of the play dramatically? In *Twelfth Night* does it similarly represent the end of Orsino's dramatic impact on events, or can we see it as the triumph of the female voice?

ACT II SCENE 5

SUMMARY

- Sir Toby gains further support against Malvolio, recruiting another member of staff, Fabian, to the cause.
- Maria leaves the letter for Malvolio to find, and they all hide to watch him read it.
- Malvolio imagines himself as a Count keeping the household in subservience.
- Malvolio is taken in by Olivia's apparent love letter, and vows to follow its instructions about his dress and demeanour, delighting the hidden onlookers.
- After he has gone, Sir Toby, Sir Andrew, Fabian and Maria look forward to seeing Malvolio present himself to Olivia according to the trick instructions.

ANALYSIS

DECEPTION AND SELF-DECEPTION

The plot to punish Malvolio for his rebukes of Sir Toby and the rest is set in motion and is supremely successful. Maria knows Malvolio better than he knows himself and the deception in her letter plays exactly to his own self-deception. It urges him to 'be opposite with a kinsman, surly with servants' (line 124), thus playing to the fantasies of advancement he exhibited from the outset, and to wear 'yellow stockings' and go 'cross-gartered' (line 127) which encourages his delusion that some chance remarks by Olivia and her 'exalted respect' (line 23) for him are a sure sign that she favours his appearance. He is thus ripe for the plot, and Fabian uses the **imagery** of snaring to describe the action: 'now is the woodcock near the gin' (line 69). The comedy of these revelations is heightened by the interjections of the onlookers. Their commentary acts as a counterpoint to Malvolio's materialistic fantasies, creating dramatic tension as they constantly threaten to interrupt him, and also a double-edged humour as they enjoy the success of his 'gulling', but also endure insults when he mentions them: 'Cousin Toby … you waste the treasure of your time with a foolish knight' (lines 57–64). Sir Toby and Sir Andrew can enjoy the joke on Malvolio, but the audience can see that the joke is on them all.

STUDY FOCUS: MALVOLIO EXPOSED A02

In this scene, Malvolio unwittingly reveals that his fantasies are not only grotesquely vain, but literally obscene. The comic effect of Maria's trick is heightened for the audience by what he immediately betrays about himself. Before he reads her letter, the morally upright steward, who has upbraided others for indulging their appetite, shows a luxurious sensuality as he imagines himself married to Olivia 'in my branched velvet gown, having come from a day-bed, where I have left Olivia sleeping' (lines 40–1). His excitement about his elevated social status is amusingly suggestive, 'wind up my watch, or play with my – some rich jewel' (lines 50–1). Letters in the title he aspires to, 'To be Count Malvolio!' (line 30), appear in his account of Olivia's handwriting – 'her very c's, her u's and her t's; and thus makes she her great p's' (lines 72–3) – which is a joke at his expense. It could be argued that the bawdiness continues to expose the physicality of his desires, **punning** on the word 'cut' for the female genitalia, and the **homophone** 'P's' = 'pees' = 'urinates'. To extend the joke Shakespeare makes the oblivious Sir Andrew literally spell it out again, 'Her c's, her u's and her t's: why that?' (line 75). Malvolio's puzzling out 'M.O.A.I' – scholars have struggled to gloss these letters – reveals the slow-wittedness accompanying his ambition. How does Malvolio's unconscious bawdiness affect the comedy of this scene? What does it reveal about Malvolio's character?

KEY QUOTATION: ACT II SCENE 5 · A01

Malvolio: 'I do not now fool myself to let imagination jade me; for every reason excites to this, that my lady loves me.' (lines 135–7)

- Malvolio's false reasoning leads him to the climactic conclusion which signals the success of Maria's device.

- Maria's letter is so successful in the deception because Malvolio was already deluding himself into thinking Olivia might marry him.

- Like other characters, Malvolio does indeed 'fool' himself, but his overweening 'sclf-love' (I.5.73) on display here means that, unlike Olivia and Orsino, he cannot be redeemed.

- The scene shows triumphantly that mistakes and devices in *Twelfth Night* are used not simply for comic effects, but to reveal underlying truths about characters and relationships.

GRADE BOOSTER · A02

It can be tempting, when exploring the text, to consider the life of characters off-stage or before or after the play begins. Doing this, one might be led to think of Maria, perhaps the most active and 'feisty' of the three female characters, being diminished by her destiny as wife of Sir Toby. However, it is best to focus on Maria's actions and speech in the play which demonstrate a ready wit, intelligence and ability to hold her own in male company.

GLOSSARY

2	**scruple**	scrap
2–3	**boiled to death**	Fabian's joke: melancholy was considered a cold humour
5	**sheep-biter**	sneaking fellow, or whoremonger
12	**metal of India**	gold
14	**behaviour**	courtly gestures
16	**contemplative**	one who stares vacantly
	Close	come close, hide
19	**tickling**	flattery: trout can be caught in shallow water by stroking them
21	**affect**	care for
27	**jets**	struts
28	**'Slight**	God's light – an oath
32	**Pistol**	shoot
36	**Jezebel**	unfaithful biblical wife (see 2 Kings 9:30–7)
37	**blows him**	puffs him up
38	**state**	chair of state
39	**stone-bow**	crossbow firing stones
40	**branched**	brocaded
44	**humour of state**	dignity of rank
44–5	**demure travel of regard**	grave look around
49	**make out**	go out
51	**curtsies**	bows
53	**Though our silence … peace!**	equivalent to 'Wild horses wouldn't draw it from me'
70	**the spirit … to him**	Toby is hoping that Malvolio will read the letter aloud
74	**contempt of question**	without a doubt
78	**impressure**	image of the seal
	Lucrece	emblem of chastity who committed suicide
80	**liver and all**	through and through
85	**numbers altered**	meter changed
87	**brock**	badger
91	**sway**	rule
92	**fustian**	cheap
96	**dressed**	prepared
97	**staniel**	kestrel
	checks	term from hawking, meaning to prepare to pounce

GLOSSARY continued

99–100 **formal capacity** normal intelligence

101 **position** arrangement

104 **Sowter** the name of a hound

108 **faults** broken trails

110 **that suffers under probation** that will stand up to scrutiny

116 **simulation** disguise

119 **revolve** consider

stars fortune and rank

123 **slough** a snake's old skin

124 **opposite** hostile

133 **champain** open country

open clear

134 **politic authors** writers on political science

baffle disgrace

135 **point-devise** in every detail

136 **jade** trick

141 **strange** aloof

stout proud

149 **sophy** ruler or Shah of Persia – probably a reference to Sir Robert Shirley who returned from the Shah in 1599 with a handsome pension

157 **play** wager

tray-trip dicing game

163 **acqua-vitae** brandy or other spirit

169 **notable contempt** public disgrace

170 **Tartar** Tartarus, the classical name for hell

CONTEXT **A04**

Cross-gartering (see line 127) was a way of fastening the garters around the leg. Depending on the exact nature of the cross-gartering, Shakespeare's audiences might have seen this as a form of ostentation from someone who is, essentially, a glorified servant, or simply as hopelessly out-of-touch with the fashions of the day.

ACT III SCENE 1

SUMMARY

- Viola and Feste exchange wordplay as she attempts to enter the house to see Olivia.
- Viola encounters Sir Toby and Sir Andrew, before Olivia and Maria come to meet Orsino's messenger.
- Olivia dismisses Maria and the knights, but then will not hear Orsino's message and declares her love for Cesario.
- Viola pities Olivia, who takes some comfort from that acknowledgement.
- Viola makes her exit saying she cannot ever love a woman.

ANALYSIS

ALONE TOGETHER

When they are on their own, the conversation of Olivia and Viola is tense with what is unspoken on both their parts. Olivia's own suppressed feelings break out at line 91 when she interrupts Viola's line, continuing the **pentameter** with her own speech. This happens again at line 95, where it is Viola who makes up Olivia's line, but is interrupted again. By picking up each other's speech **rhythms** and echoing certain words and phrases, a brisk interchange is indicated and intimacy is suggested. Viola, it seems, has made two strong attachments – to Orsino and Olivia – while in her disguise. Olivia's following speech gives some indications of her heightened emotional state: there are many **caesuras**, a **hypermetric** line (105) and the whole speech, in strained **syntax**, is studded with questions and the pronouns 'I' and 'you'. Olivia's diction is fervent: 'shameful cunning', 'baited', 'unmuzzled thoughts', 'tyrannous' (lines 101–5) – and the burden of this outburst seems to be to blame Cesario for the situation.

STIFLED EMOTIONS

The clock interrupts Olivia's concentration (see **Part Three: Themes**, on **Twelfth Night**), but she returns, more urgently than before, to her questioning of Viola. The interchange of single lines (its technical term is **stichomythia**) has a real energy of repressed passion: again, neither woman is able to speak her feelings. There is a kind of desperation in Olivia's 'I would you were as I would have you be' (line 127): having dedicated herself to mourning, she is suddenly overwhelmed by her desires. Orsino warned that she had a great capacity for love if she would only let herself (I.1.33–40): now the force of that stifled emotion has taken hold of Olivia. Both characters speak in end-rhymed verse at the end of the scene, from line 132 onwards. Perhaps this represents a kind of **metaphorical** breathing space from the heightened situation within the confines of rhyme; perhaps it is a way of controlling and curbing a conversation which has become uncomfortably intense. That Viola picks up this form too suggests her responsiveness to Olivia – perhaps this is one of the subtle aspects of Cesario's conversation which has so attracted the Countess. Viola can only extricate herself with a kind of verbal trickery worthy of Feste, but all the while she engages in this double-speak, whether with Orsino or Olivia, she maintains her essential integrity, concluding here directly and sincerely that regarding her own self no woman shall ever 'mistress be of it, save I alone' (line 145). This intense scene is the height of the relationship between Olivia and Viola (see **Extended Commentary: Act III Scene 1 lines 96–149**); they meet alone once more and only briefly. Consider how Shakespeare maintains the erotic intensity between the two women, whilst ensuring that it does not become too painful or cruel for comedy.

> **CHECK THE PLAY** **A03**
>
> In *As You like It* (III.5), Rosalind, disguised as a boy Ganymede, attracts Phebe who is being wooed by Silvius, a shepherd. Compare Phebe's attitude to the shepherd, 'I shall not pity thee', and the mocking way Rosalind then treats Phebe, 'Sell when you can; you are not for all markets', with the way Viola behaves towards Olivia in this scene.

CONTEXT A04

Feste's **metaphor** for a sentence is a glove, expressing the malleability of language. Shakespeare's father John was a glover who made fine goatskin (cheveril) gloves for ladies and signed his name with a pair of glover's compasses. Perhaps it is not accidental that the **image** Feste uses here for a sentence, which it is Shakespeare's job to manipulate, is a goatskin glove, a reference to his father's trade.

STUDY FOCUS: FOOLING WITH WORDS A02

Wordplay, and the gap between words and their meanings, or words and proper communication, are all much in evidence here. Feste's **punning** begins the scene, and he shows how, as in Act I Scene 5, 'foolery' can have a serious **satiric** purpose. He equates fools and husbands (lines 28–9), and also makes a comment about Jove sending the clean-cut young Cesario 'a beard' (line 38), a pointed observation sometimes taken to indicate that he knows the truth of the disguise. Feste sums up his role as 'corrupter of words' (line 30); Viola observes that he 'is wise enough to play the fool' (line 50). Feste argues that a sentence is 'but a cheveril glove to a good wit' (lines 9–10), easily turned inside out. This twisting of language is characteristic of the misapprehensions in the scene which follows, but Feste sees language itself, our very means of constructing reason, as debased, rendering reason also uncertain: 'I can yield you none without words, and words are grown so false I am loath to prove reason with them' (lines 20–1).

As a number of characters look set to be made fools of (or make fools of themselves) – Malvolio, Orsino, Olivia, Viola, Sir Andrew – definitions of 'fooling' and 'folly' become acute. Feste also makes the link between verbal dexterity and sex, picking up the erotic implications of Viola's word 'dally' (line 12) and applying it to the word 'sister' as a 'wanton' (lines 16–17), and this may be associated with Viola's suggestive description of Olivia's 'most pregnant and vouchsafed ear' (lines 74–5). He then uses wordplay to link sex to money, 'Would not a pair of these have bred, sir?' (line 41). Viola's response, 'Yes, being kept together and put to use' (line 42), picks up the link and takes it further. The scene also shows how erotic desire expresses itself in language in the exchange between Olivia and Viola. It is no surprise that amid these word games Viola calls herself Olivia's 'fool' (line 129). Examine in detail how the wordplay works in this scene. What effect does it have on the mood of the scene before the second meeting between Viola and Olivia?

VIOLA'S SOLILOQUY

Viola's jesting wordplay with Feste is in prose, but she has a short, philosophical **soliloquy** in verse at lines 50–8, which continues the theme of overlapping wisdom and folly. She is more than a match for the two knights, trumping Sir Andrew's French greeting (line 61) with a prompt and fluent reply, and conducting alert verbal jousting with Sir Toby, an exchange itself perhaps involving innuendo with the play on 'enter' and 'entrance' (lines 65–71).

GLOSSARY

1	**live by**	make a living from
1	**tabor**	small drum
12	**dally nicely**	play subtly
13	**wanton**	(a) equivocal, (b) unchaste
18	**bonds disgraced**	legal contracts disgraced a man's honesty by implying his word was not to be trusted
36	**pass upon**	jest at
38	**commodity**	supply
42	**use**	interest
43	**Pandarus**	the go-between the lovers in the medieval story of *Troilus and Cressida*
	conster	construe
48–9	**out of my welkin**	not my business
49	**element**	sky, or one of the four elements
54	**haggard**	hawk
	feather	bird
58	**folly-fallen**	fallen into folly
61–2	*Dieu vous … serviteur*	(French) God keep you sir! And you too; your servant
64	**encounter**	approach, enter
66	**list**	goal
67	**Taste**	try out
74	**pregnant**	receptive
75	**vouchsafed**	attentive
83	**'Twas never merry world**	equivalent to 'Things have never been the same'
84	**lowly feigning**	pretence of humility
94	**music from the spheres**	ancient astrology held that the heavens made music as they moved
100	**construction**	interpretation
103–4	**at the stake … thoughts**	the images are from bear-baiting
105	**receiving**	perception
106	**cypress**	veil of black gauze
109	**grise**	flight of steps
	vulgar proof	common experience
118	**proper**	handsome
119	**due west**	used metaphorically to dismiss Cesario to seek his fortune elsewhere, perhaps with melancholic associations
	westward ho!	call for passengers by Thames boatmen going to Westminster
133	**Love's night is noon**	love cannot be hidden
136	**maugre**	despite
138	**clause**	promise
139	**For that**	because

GRADE BOOSTER **A02**

It is important to bear in mind that there are some ideas which are particularly relevant to *Twelfth Night*; the issue of wisdom and folly is one of these. Being 'wise' can be seen as a great leveller within the play – in that aristocrats, Olivia and Orsino, are seen to be foolish when it comes to feeling, whilst Feste, Viola and Maria – all servants at least superficially – show wisdom and wit. Consider where you would place other characters on the scale between folly, at one end, and wisdom at the other.

EXTENDED COMMENTARY

ACT III SCENE 1 LINES 96–149

When they last met, Viola called the shots and dominated the conversation (see **Extended Commentary: Act I Scene 5 lines 139–207**). Here the tables are turned and it is Olivia who is setting the pace. Her first speech is full of condemnation of herself and, by implication, of Cesario for her previous behaviour in sending after him with a ring. Their earlier meeting is described as 'the last enchantment' (line 97). Olivia's sense of being entrapped by her sudden love for Orsino's messenger is conveyed in the **image** of herself as a bear 'at the stake' (line 103). Her speech is expressive of confused and passionate feeling, with **rhetorical** questions, a **hypermetric** line suggesting thoughts which cannot be contained by the regular **iambic pentameter** (line 105), and heavy punctuation in the middle of lines giving a jerky feel to the flow of the verse. Olivia moves from blaming herself for her own 'shameful cunning' (line 101) to blaming Cesario for having cruelly 'baited' her heart (line 104).

After this long outburst of pent-up and unaccustomed feeling, Viola's response is brief: 'I pity you' (line 108). Olivia is so desperate that she seizes on this as positive evidence of Cesario's feelings for her, but Viola quickly disabuses her of that comfort: 'very oft we pity enemies' (line 110). Olivia responds with more animal imagery (lines 113–14) in a speech of self-mockery. The intrusion of the clock shifts the intensity into a different key. Olivia's sudden awareness of 'the waste of time' (line 115) seems less about the immediate situation than a remark about her wider circumstances, committed to spending her own youth in long mourning. This realisation seems to cause her to try to relax her emotional grip on Cesario, 'I will not have you' (line 116), predicting instead some later marriage, but her effort is futile. There is a desperation in Olivia's sudden command 'Stay!', this single word being marked with its own line (122), and the abrupt and pleading question, 'I prithee tell me what thou think'st of me?' (line 123), which inaugurates a quick sequence of responses between the two in a rhetorical exchange known technically as **stichomythia**. The sentences themselves are like a flourish of Feste's wit, prickling with **syntactical** and logical **paradoxes** about the gaps between seeming, being and knowing. Both women are divided from themselves: Olivia, because of her overpowering feelings for another woman, and Viola because she can only ever allude to her true self in enigmatic formulae such as 'I am not what I am' (line 126), this last producing an impassioned monosyllabic line from Olivia, in which she plays on the verb, her desire being expressed in the grammatical gap between the present 'am', the subjunctive 'were' and the infinitive 'be': 'I would you were as I would have you be' (line 127).

Cesario cannot return Olivia's feeling, but the intensity of her engagement is revealed in her anger. Shakespeare is careful to ensure that the scene remains comic, however, by using humour as a safety valve, for instance in Olivia's **aside** admiring 'his' countenance and he avoids the danger of cruelty by making clear that Viola pities Olivia and remains sincere rather than manipulative in her disguise. The emotional conflict prompts an outright declaration: 'I love thee so' (line 136). Olivia uses here the intimate 'thee' form. Viola's reply is cryptic and yet blunt and honest: 'I have one heart, one bosom, and one truth,/ And that no woman has; nor never none/ Shall mistress be of it, save I alone' (lines 142–5). The retreat into **rhyming couplets** which began with Olivia's avowal of love at line 136 seems to suggest a kind of deliberateness of expression, a desire not to be misunderstood, in a formal, deep-breath kind of delivery. Yet everything she has just said makes it clear that Olivia, despite Cesario's absolute refusal, cannot take no for an answer: she remains undeterred by the vehemence of Cesario's response, inviting him to continue his efforts to woo her for Orsino. Consider how Shakespeare uses this meeting between the two women to show the impossibility of Viola, as Cesario, ever resolving the situation with Olivia.

CHECK THE PLAY **A03**

A vivid comparison can be drawn between *Twelfth Night* and the play *La Fausse Suivante* (The False Servant) by the French eighteenth-century dramatist Pierre de Marivaux (see the 2004 translation by Martin Crimp) in which a young Parisian woman dresses as a man to establish the fidelity of her prospective husband. In her disguise she woos a Countess and, in an extraordinary scene (III.6), full of wit and verbal dexterity, in contrast to the compassionate approach in *Twelfth Night*, the erotic interplay between the two women is taken to an extreme, almost sadistic pitch.

ACT III SCENE 2

SUMMARY

- Sir Andrew is aggrieved that Olivia favours Cesario, and threatens to leave.
- Aided by Fabian, Sir Toby persuades Sir Andrew that Olivia favours him.
- Sir Andrew goes to write to Cesario to challenge him to a duel.
- Maria enters with the news that Malvolio is wearing cross-garters and yellow stockings.

ANALYSIS

SIR ANDREW THE 'RIVAL'

Sir Andrew Aguecheek joins the ranks of those in the play who are unlucky, unhappy or unrequited in love. His departure would cut off Sir Toby's money supply and bring his revelry to an end, so Fabian and Sir Toby raise the stakes by encouraging him to the duel, despite having apparently little regard for his martial qualities: 'awake your dormouse valour' (line 15). From the outset there has been more than a hint that Sir Toby's greed is his prime motive for his friendship with Sir Andrew, perhaps anticipating his explicit cruelty in Act V Scene 1. Many critics and theatre directors have felt that the play's **rhythm** falters with this long scene, but the 'gulling' of Sir Andrew is critical to much of the sub-plot, including the trick against Malvolio (which would never have happened without his late-night rollicking with Sir Toby) and he now becomes an agent in the main plot as a result of the duel, which, although comic, puts Viola under pressure in her disguise as Cesario.

GRADE BOOSTER A02

The scene is enlivened by the vigorous speech of, for example, Fabian, 'you are now sailed into the north of my lady's opinion, where you will hang like an icicle on a Dutchman's beard' (lines 20–2), and later Maria, 'He does smile himself into more lines than is in the new map with the augmentation of the Indies' (lines 61–3). Through a close analysis of the language, show how Shakespeare's prose ensures that the scene maintains an engaging vitality which whets our eagerness for the comical sights to come.

GLOSSARY

12	**grand-jurymen**	the jurors deciding whether there was sufficient evidence for a case to go to a full trial
19	**double gilt**	twice-gilded (of gold), therefore, twice as lucky
21	**north of my lady's opinion**	disfavour, coldness
22	**Dutchman's beard perhaps**	an allusion to William Barentz who led an expedition to the Arctic in 1596–7
25	**Brownist**	member of an extreme Puritan group founded by Robert Browne and advocating the separation of church and state
26	**me**	on my advice
35	**'thou'est him**	call him 'thou', as a social inferior
37	**bed of Ware**	a famous Elizabethan bed, now in the V&A museum in London (see page 42)
38	**gall**	(a) bitterness, (b) ingredient of ink
41	**cubiculo**	Toby's affected Italian word for 'bedroom'
47	**wainropes**	wagon-ropes pulled by oxen
	hale	haul, drag
49	**anatomy**	corpse
53	**the spleen**	a fit of laughter, thought to come from the spleen
56	**impossible passages of grossness**	wildly unlikely statements
62–3	**the new map ... Indies**	a new map by Emmeric Mollineux published in 1599 drew the East Indies more fully than previously

(see page 42)

The theory of the four humours produced a type of Elizabethan comedy in which each character is governed by one of them, such as *Every Man in His Humour* (1599) by Ben Jonson. In *Twelfth Night*, however, characters are not fixed 'types', but individuals dealing with their own delusions, appetites and desires. As Sir Toby says earlier to Sir Andrew, 'Does not our lives consist of the four elements?' (II.2.7–8), to which Sir Andrew replies, 'Faith, so they say, but I think it rather consists of eating and drinking' (lines 9–10).

KEY QUOTATION: ACT III SCENE 2 **A01**

Sir Toby: 'For Andrew, if he were opened and you find so much blood in his liver as will clog the foot of a flea, I'll eat the rest of the anatomy.' (lines 48–9)

● Sir Toby does not believe that Sir Andrew has the courage to fight Cesario.

● The 'gulling' of Sir Andrew is treated in detail, as one of the many games and tricks where false appearances lead to comic confusion and also because it places Viola's masquerade under threat.

● The liver was linked with blood, one of the four humours, and was associated, among other things, with lust; Sir Toby makes one of the many references to the liver in the play, another one being by Fabian earlier in the scene (line 16) and the first by Orsino when talking of Olivia (I.1.37).

● When she enters this scene, Maria relates the progress in the revenge against Malvolio in terms of the 'spleen', the organ producing another of the four humours; this **image** is appropriate to the revenge against the yellow-stockinged Malvolio, since the spleen was linked with 'yellow' bile and a vengeful nature.

ACT III SCENE 3

SUMMARY

- Out of concern and devotion, Antonio has followed Sebastian.
- Sebastian is grateful for Antonio's care.
- Antonio confesses that he had previously been in a seafight with Orsino's men and so is at risk of arrest in Illyria.
- To avoid trouble he goes to an inn, leaving his purse for Sebastian's convenience.

ANALYSIS

ANTONIO'S LOVE

The scene reminds us about Sebastian. It comes just before Viola faces her 'duel' and so reassures the audience, as did Sir Toby's comments about Sir Andrew's lack of valour, that, despite the apparent danger, she will survive and a solution to her predicament is near. The scene also stresses the intensity of Antonio's bond with Sebastian, as the older man seeks to protect and care for his young companion. The information about Antonio's past dealings with the Illyrians shows that he has put himself in great danger by following him; it could be argued that Antonio is the only character in the play who acts selflessly in the service of someone he loves (see **Part Three: Characters**). Sebastian, by contrast, seems rid of the burden of grief which **characterised** his previous appearance. His speeches are brief – perhaps indicative of embarrassment. The repetition of 'thanks' (lines 14 and 15) may suggest he does not know how to respond to the persistence of Antonio's devotion, or that he simply cannot find a way to thank Antonio. He is quickly, however, on to lighter topics, keen to go sightseeing, unperturbed by Antonio's revelations and perhaps immaturely fascinated at an older man's tales of adventures: 'Belike you slew great number of his people?' (line 29). The nature of Antonio's past crimes is not made clear, and there is some discrepancy between his dismissal of Sebastian's curiosity about killings – 'Th'offence is not of such a bloody nature' (line 30) – and the later account of events in Act V Scene 1.

GLOSSARY

6	**not all**	not only
8	**jealousy**	concern
9	**skilless in**	unacquainted with
12	**rather**	more quickly
16	**uncurrent**	not legal tender
17	**conscience**	sense of indebtedness
24	**renown**	make famous
26	**count his**	count's
28	**tane**	captured
	scarce be answered	difficult to make reparation
31	**quality**	circumstances
34	**traffic**	trade
36	**lapsèd**	apprehended
44	**Haply**	perhaps
45	**your store**	your money
46	**idle markets**	unnecessary expenditure

CONTEXT   **A04**

The Elephant (line 49) was the name of an inn near the Globe Theatre in Southwark. Shakespeare interweaves other local and contemporary references into the world of Illyria to give it immediacy. Trace some of these other references made through the play to local places or events.

ACT III SCENE 4

SUMMARY

CHECK THE PLAY **A03**

Viola is keen to pacify her opponent, as is Sir Andrew, but the two unwilling parties are brought to the brink of fighting by Sir Toby's provocations, presumably for his own amusement. Shakespeare makes use of a similar joke in *The Merry Wives of Windsor* in the duel between Sir Hugh, the Welsh priest, and Caius, the French doctor (III.1), which is engineered by the Host, Shallow and Master Page. Compare the two scenes and note the dramatic techniques, such as **soliloquies** and **asides**, Shakespeare uses to maintain the comic mood.

- Maria suggests to Olivia that Malvolio is 'possessed'.
- Olivia, thinking of Cesario, is greeted by the sight of a smiling, yellow-stockinged, cross-gartered Malvolio.
- Olivia tells him to go to bed to recover, which Malvolio takes as a sexual invitation, and he quotes from Maria's letter so that Olivia concludes that he has gone mad.
- Olivia goes to meet Cesario, leaving Malvolio convinced she will marry him.
- Misinterpreting Olivia's mention of Sir Toby, Malvolio is rude to him, and, after Malvolio has gone, Sir Toby promises the conspirators to continue their joke.
- Sir Andrew's challenge to Cesario is read out, but after Sir Andrew leaves, Sir Toby tells Fabian he won't deliver the letter because it is comical. He decides to deliver a challenge by word of mouth instead so as to strike fear into Cesario.
- Viola returns at Olivia's command, but only to ask her to love Orsino.
- Sir Toby tells Cesario that Sir Andrew wants a duel with Cesario.
- Sir Toby encourages Sir Andrew to fight Cesario; Antonio enters and thinks it is Sebastian who is in danger.
- Before Antonio can do anything he is arrested, and he appeals to 'Sebastian' for help, but Viola replies that she does not know him.
- After Antonio has been taken away, Viola wonders whether the mystery might mean that Sebastian is still alive.

ANALYSIS

'THE FRUITS OF THE SPORT'

A number of plots come together in this long climactic scene, in which each of the nine characters is to some degree deluded or ignorant of the total situation, leaving the audience to enjoy the increasing mania of the action, or what Maria has called the 'fruits of the sport' (II.5.164). Maria's scheme against Malvolio culminates in the steward making a fool of himself in front of Olivia and the rest of the household. A more immediate risk to Viola's masculine disguise is the manufactured threat from Sir Andrew, exacerbated by Sir Toby, who describes the timid knight as 'full of despite, bloody as the hunter' (lines 188–9). The parallel plots of the twins connect in Antonio's mistaking of Viola for Sebastian, which lays the ground for Olivia's same error, and the hope this gives Viola that Sebastian is not drowned takes the plot a good step towards resolution. Getting all these intrigues working together involves complex stage-management, and Shakespeare is aware of the danger that the action might seem implausible. As Fabian wryly notes, 'If this were played upon a stage now, I could condemn it as an improbable fiction' (lines 108–9). By pre-empting our disbelief, the play makes a virtue of its machinations, leaving the audience to delight in the theatricality of the mix-ups and antics.

'SAD AND MERRY MADNESSS'

Malvolio's humiliation is not subtle, but is often extremely funny when played in the theatre. The contrast between the uptight 'Puritan' of the earlier scenes and the grinning, lascivious fashion victim of this scene is pointed (see **Part Three: Characters**) and Olivia's conclusion that this catalogue of bizarre comments is 'very midsummer madness' (line 50) gives the plotters an idea of how to continue the torture of their victim. Olivia herself notes that Malvolio's apparent madness is an acute example of the way in which a number of the characters make fools of themselves and identifies herself with it: 'I am as mad as he/ If sad and merry madness equal be' (lines 14–15). Note some of the many references to madness in *Twelfth Night* (and see **Part Three: Themes**, on **Madness**). Consider how the play's 'sad and merry madness' turns the world of Illyria upside down and so by extension challenges the accepted norms of the audience.

STUDY FOCUS: THE PANGS OF LAUGHTER A02

After the passionate exchanges of Act III Scene 1, the meeting here between Olivia and Viola, a short verse interlude amid the increasingly frenzied action, is strained and painful. Olivia gives a kind of apology for her behaviour, 'I have said too much unto a heart of stone' (line 168), but Viola's terse reply immediately prompts desperation in Olivia. At the start of Act III, Feste had made a parallel between Olivia and Cesario and

Troilus and Cressida, adding 'Cressida was a beggar' (III.1.47), and here we see Olivia in frantic half lines, begging Cesario to receive her picture: 'Here, wear this jewel for me; 'tis my picture./ Refuse it not; it hath no tongue to vex you./ And, I beseech you, come again tomorrow' (lines 175–8). They do not meet again until the last scene and never alone. Viola is then placed in what she believes to be mortal danger and while the audience knows this is false, her own desperation is clear: 'I am one that had rather go with sir priest than sir knight' (lines 229–30). Her aside, 'a little thing would make me tell them how much I lack of a man' (lines 255–6), while being a shared joke with the audience, with a bawdy **pun** on precisely what 'little thing' of a man's it is she lacks (see **Part Three: Themes**, on **Gender**), is also an expression of fear and shows how close she comes to revealing her disguise. Identify key points in the scene which the characters perceive as dangerous, threatening or painful. How does Shakespeare maintain the comic balance of laughter and concern in the audience?

ANTONIO'S AGONY

Antonio's intervention in the scene brings with it a note of potential tragedy. His denunciations in verse of the apparent ingratitude of his friend Sebastian are based on a misunderstanding, but they also **foreshadow** the way in which his kindnesses will be increasingly eclipsed by other, more pressing relationships in the rest of the play. He rails, in a slightly disconnected vein, on the 'beauteous evil' of Sebastian's outward appearance, which promises good but hides an inner blemish (lines 316–21): the language of idolatry – 'idol', 'god' – expresses the strength, perhaps the excessive strength, of his emotions (see **Part Three: Themes**, on **Excess**, and **Love and self-love**). His pain and rage are a reminder that the seductive charm of youth can bring with it unwitting cruelty and carries potentially tragic dangers for an older lover. Interestingly, his portrayal of a man he believes to be Sebastian highlights a disparity between external and internal appearance, and is thus an appropriate description of the disguised Viola herself. The speech is a darker version of Viola's own 'disguise, I see thou art a wickedness' (II.1.24). It is only when Viola is mistaken for Sebastian that she reveals that she has fashioned her disguise on his appearance: 'I my brother know/ Yet living in my glass; even such and so/ In favour was my brother, and he went/ Still in this fashion, colour, ornament,/ For him I imitate' (lines 330–4). Thus retrospectively she gives a reason for her adoption of male clothes in the first place: as a symptom of grief and a way of keeping the supposedly dead sibling 'alive'. The possibility that her twin brother might not be dead after all comes as a sudden and welcome idea at the end of the confusion, and so finally the 'knot' (II.2.33) of the plot's complications begins to untangle. The scene brings together the comic devices of the main and sub-plots, but it also combines strains of feeling involving fear, pain and rage.

CHECK THE PLAY A03

In the RSC modern-dress production of 2012, the lack of subtlety in Malvolio's humiliation was taken to its extreme in a grotesque transformation in which Jonathan Slinger wore women's underwear and a codpiece. In complete contrast, the BBC production (1980) made little of the physical transformation and instead kept Alec McCowen's face in close-up to magnify a psychologically subtle and compelling portrayal of self-delusion.

GRADE BOOSTER A01

One of the ways Shakespeare is able to combine such an exhilirating diversity of actions and feelings within one scene is to deploy a wide range of language forms, including prose speech, letters, **blank verse**, half lines and **rhyming couplets**. Analyse the scene in terms of its dramatic language and find when and consider why Shakespeare shifts from one form to another.

GLOSSARY

5	**sad and civil**	grave and respectful
21–2	**'Please one and please all'**	the refrain of a popular bawdy ballad of the time
24	**black in my mind**	theory held that melancholy was caused by excess black bile
26	**Roman hand**	newly fashionable italic handwriting
28	**Ay … thee**	another quotation from a bawdy ballad
58	**come near me**	begin to understand who I am
66	**limed**	snared
70	**incredulous**	incredible
75	**Legion**	used of the devils possessing the madman in Mark 5:9.
98	**bawcock**	fine bird
100	**biddy**	shortened form of chickabiddy, hen
	gravity	a man of dignity
101	**cherry-pit**	children's game of throwing cherry stones into a hole
106	**element**	sphere
110	**genius**	soul
111	**take air, and taint**	be spoilt through exposure (it was believed that fresh air was bad for fevers)
114	**dark room and bound**	the usual treatment for madness
118	**to the bar**	into the open
123	**saucy**	(a) impudent, (b) spicy
132	**in thy throat**	deeply
139	**windy side**	safe side
149	**bumbaily**	contemptuous term for a bailiff (because they crept up on debtors from behind)
152	**proof**	trial
158	**clodpole**	blockhead
163	**cockatrices**	mythical monsters able to kill with a look
164	**give them way**	keep out of their way
175	**jewel**	jewelled miniature painting
179	**honour … give**	that can be granted without compromising my honour (i.e. virginity)
189	**despite**	defiance
190	**Dismount thy tuck**	draw thy sword
	yare	prompt
200–1	**carpet consideration**	courtly rather than military reasons
204	**Hob nob**	come what may
205	**conduct**	escort
209	**competent**	to be reckoned with
213	**meddle**	duel
221–2	**mortal arbitrement**	trial by combat to the death
232	**firago**	virago, fighting woman
233	**pass**	duelling bout
	pays	kills, finishes
245	**perdition of souls**	killing
260	**duello**	code of duelling
270	**undertaker**	one who undertakes a duel on another's behalf
279	**favour**	face
296	**my present**	what I have at present
299	**deserts**	services deserving of reward
329	**saws**	sayings
343	**event**	result

ACT IV SCENE 1

SUMMARY

- Feste greets Sebastian as Cesario, with the message for him to return to Olivia.
- Sir Andrew also mistakes Sebastian for his twin and hits him.
- Sebastian defends himself and, in the fight, Sir Andrew is bettered by his adversary.
- Olivia enters to see Sir Toby and Sebastian square up to each other.
- Olivia chastises Sir Toby for his behaviour and takes Sebastian to her house.

ANALYSIS

AN ANSWER FOR OLIVIA

This scene introduces Olivia to the male twin who will resolve her passionate attraction to Cesario, and, although the exchange between her and Sebastian is brief, in two rhyming couplets we are given to understand that Sebastian is quite happy with the attentions of this unknown woman (lines 53–6). Feste's misunderstanding serves to bring the pair together, and, incidentally to prompt Olivia to some harsh words to her layabout uncle Sir Toby. The words 'fool' 'folly' and 'foolish' which are bandied around between Sebastian and Feste highlight the absurdity of a disordered situation which is coming to a resolution.

STUDY FOCUS: 'NOTHING THAT IS SO, IS SO' | A02

When Sebastian denies that he is the object of Feste's errand, his language is the **idiom** of fooling: 'thou art a foolish fellow' (line 2). Feste responds with a knowing series of negatives, which are **ironically** all true, and concludes 'Nothing that is so, is so' (lines 6–7), which is more than merely an apt summary of the reigning confusions of the plot, but encapsulates the topsy-turvy world of Illyria in which reality itself is brought into doubt, leaving a realm of uncertainty and possibility. As Viola has already stated, 'I am not that I play' (I.5.153). In Illyria, the self, and more specifically the different gender roles which are the root of identity, are not fixed, but are shifting. One indication of this movement is in Viola's own references to her self: 'I am a gentleman' (I.5.233), 'I am the man … As I am man … As I am woman' (II.2.22, 33 and 35), 'were I a woman' (II.4.104), 'I am all the daughters … and all the brothers too' (II.4.116–17) and 'I am not what I am' (III.1.126). Explore how Shakespeare uses Viola's transvestite disguise and the identical twins to create comic possibilities in identities, situations and relationships.

GLOSSARY

4	**held out**	kept up
12	**cockney**	one using affected language
15	**foolish Greek**	buffoon
19–20	**fourteen years' purchase**	since Elizabethan land prices were usually twelve times the annual rent, this means a large sum
37	**malapert**	impudent
44	**Rudesby**	ruffian
46	**extent**	assault
53	**What relish is in this?**	What does this mean?
55	**Lethe**	mythical river inducing oblivion

CHECK THE PLAY | A03

Of course, by virtue of their sex, male and female twins can never be completely identical, but the 2002 Globe production showed how, in an all-male production, the theatrical illusion could make the twins indistinguishable on stage and so create a real confusion in the audience as well as the characters. How would such a dramatic effect change the way the audience might perceive the scenes in which Sebastian appears?

ACT IV SCENE 2

SUMMARY

- Feste disguises himself as a learned priest, Sir Topas, and adopts a different voice.
- He taunts the imprisoned Malvolio in front of Maria and Sir Toby, trying to make Malvolio believe he is mad.
- Sir Toby wants to end the joke because he is falling out of favour with Olivia, and leaves with Maria.
- Feste returns in his own guise as fool and continues to torment Malvolio.
- The steward asks for pen and paper to write to Olivia about his treatment.
- Feste promises to return and departs singing and jesting.

ANALYSIS

CRUEL CONFINEMENT

The plot against Malvolio takes on a darker aspect with the new involvement of Feste, not previously part of the scheming, but the antagonist of Malvolio from the first moment they appear together (I.5.60–5). The treatment of Malvolio in this scene brings out the latent cruelty inherent in comedy, and offers a darker perspective on Feste's role (see **Part Three: Characters**). Nevertheless, while other characters progress beyond their self-delusions towards love of another, Malvolio goes the opposite way. Orsino escapes his love canopy of flowers and Olivia her cloister of grief, but Malvolio's vanity leads him from his self-confinement in yellow stockings and cross-garters, where he is exactly a laughing-stock, to his literal imprisonment in a dungeon of isolation and darkness and, finally, to his exclusion from the confines of the comedy itself. Malvolio fails to perceive what love makes Olivia realise immediately when she exclaims, 'ourselves we do not owe' (I.5.265).

The development of these characters seems to suggest that, if this is so, wisdom and humanity lie in abandoning the self – or, as Olivia puts it, 'Let it be' (I.5.253), or again, 'What is decreed must be; and be this so' (I.5.266) – while the effort and strictures of rigid self-possession lead to insanity. The play's insistent questioning of categories of madness and sanity, or wisdom and folly (see **Part Three: Themes**, on **Madness**) is therefore brought to the fore in this scene. 'I am as well in my wits, fool, as thou art', says a frightened Malvolio. 'Then you are mad indeed, if you be no better in your wits than a fool', is Feste's unpitying retort (lines 73–6). Feste's disguise as Sir Topas is also significant as a harsher version of the deceits practised elsewhere in the play, which discover truth.

GRADE BOOSTER A03

Directors often use modern-day settings for Shakespeare's plays so as to highlight their social, political and cultural relevance, but such choices need to serve the play. If you were staging *Twelfth Night*, what setting and costumes would you choose and why?

FESTE'S 'FOOLOSOPHY'

As Sir Topas, Feste's 'foolosophy' becomes literal as he catechises Malvolio on Pythagoras's theory of the transmigration of souls, *metempsychosis*. Malvolio rejects the idea, but Sir Topas requires him to accept it to be acknowledged as sane. The selection of this topic might appear random and nonsensical, but it could be seen to have a strange resonance not only here, but in the play as a whole, since love comes close to being expressed in terms of a union of souls. In answer to how she would pursue her love, Viola tells Olivia she would 'call upon my soul within the house' (I.5.224); it is at this very point that Olivia falls in love with her. When the twins are reunited Sebastian asks of Viola, 'Do I stand there?' (V.1.210), and in his final speech Orsino pledges that 'A solemn combination shall be made/ Of our dear souls' (V.1.360–1). We could argue that Malvolio is physically imprisoned, but his self-absorption also confines him spiritually in a dungeon of the self, leaving his soul unable to 'migrate' to another in love.

REVISION FOCUS: TASK 2   A02

How far do you agree with the following statements?

- Malvolio's treatment at the hands of Feste and Sir Toby goes beyond reasonable revenge.
- 'Fool' is a particularly inappropriate term for Feste in this scene.

Try writing opening paragraphs for essays based on these discussion points. Set out your arguments clearly.

CONTEXT   A04

Transmigration is not a belief unique to Pythagoras and is one shared, to a greater or lesser extent, by religious systems such as Buddhism and Hinduism. It is interesting to reflect on how the exchange between Malvolio and 'Sir Topas' would have been received by Shakespearean audiences who, whilst no doubt tending towards the rational, Christian explanation advanced by Malvolio, would also have accepted the idea of someone being possessed by evil spirits – in its own way, a transmigration, albeit of a different sort.

GLOSSARY

2	**Topas**	the topaz stone was believed to cure lunacy
7	**said**	called
8	**a good housekeeper**	hospitable
	careful	conscientious
9	**competitors**	partners-in-crime
11	*Bonos dies*	good day, in mock Latin
	hermit of Prague	this seems to be a bogus scholarly authority invented by Feste
12	**Gorboduc**	king of ancient Britain, subject of the earliest English tragedy (1561)
28	**house**	a room
30	**barricadoes**	barricades
31	**clerestories**	high windows
35	**Egyptians in their fog**	a plague of darkness was visited on the Egyptians in Exodus 10:21–3
38	**constant question**	logical discussion
40	**Pythagoras**	Ancient Greek philosopher who held that the soul could inhabit different bodies in succession (the theory of transmigration)
50	**I am for all waters**	I can turn my hand to anything
61	**perdy**	by God (corruption of *par Dieu*)
72	**five wits**	the five faculties were wit, imagination, fantasy, estimation and memory
77	**propertied me**	treated me like a piece of furniture
78	**face**	bully
80	**Advise you**	be careful
88	**shent**	scolded
92	**Well-a-day**	Alas
106	**old Vice**	predecessor of the Elizabethan stage fool in earlier morality dramas
112	**Pare thy nails**	a piece of stage business for the Vice
	dad	some plays cast the Vice as the son of the devil

PITAGORA

ACT IV SCENE 3

SUMMARY

- Sebastian wonders at the turn of events.
- Olivia brings a priest to Sebastian to confirm their marriage, saying they can keep it a secret.
- Sebastian agrees and they go to the chapel.

ANALYSIS

A BAFFLED SEBASTIAN

GRADE BOOSTER **A01**

Sebastian tries to rationalise his situation, his mental effort clear in the **syntax**, with the conjunctions 'yet', 'though', 'but', 'or', 'that' and 'as' developing and linking his train of thought. Analyse Sebastian's soliloquy in detail showing how he tries to use logic to convince himself that he and Olivia are not mad.

In contrast to the darkness of Malvolio's cell, this scene opens with Sebastian's reference to the 'glorious sun' (line 1). Sebastian's **soliloquy** reviews Olivia's treatment of him and it seems he can hardly believe his luck: ''tis wonder that enwraps me thus ... not madness'

(lines 3–4). His rapid assent to a proposal of marriage from a beautiful woman he has hardly met may seem surprising (see **Part Three: Characters**) and the poet W. H. Auden felt this sudden and unprompted acceptance reflected badly on him, but Sebastian's soliloquy does show him bewildered by events. Like many other characters in the play he wonders if he is mad, repeated at lines 4, 10 and 15, or whether it is 'the lady' (he never calls her by her name: presumably he does not know it) who is 'mad' (line 16). On this last point, Sebastian concludes that she could not manage her household were she insane (see **Part Three: Themes**, on **Madness**). His wish for Antonio's advice shows how much he, like Viola, is alone in this extraordinary situation. The substitution of Sebastian for 'Cesario' in Olivia's hastily arranged marriage has a pleasing symmetry, perhaps exemplified in the two **rhyming couplets** which conclude the scene (lines 32–5).

GLOSSARY

12	**discourse**	reasoning
17	**sway**	rule
18	**dispatch**	orders
21	**deceivable**	deceptive
24	**chantry by**	nearby chapel, where masses for the souls of the dead were said
26	**Plight me the full assurance**	a betrothal in front of a priest was as legally binding as a full marriage service
29	**Whiles**	until
31	**birth**	nobility

ACT V SCENE 1

SUMMARY

- Fabian and Feste discuss the letter Feste agreed to deliver for the imprisoned Malvolio.
- Orsino and Viola arrive and Orsino engages in banter with Feste over money.
- Antonio is brought in and Orsino recognises him as a pirate, but Antonio denies this, saying he and Sebastian have been companions for three months.
- When Olivia arrives she continues to reject Orsino and greets Cesario warmly. Orsino asks why he should not kill Olivia and then, because he knows she loves Cesario, he threatens to kill his servant.
- Viola accepts such a fate and is about to leave with Orsino when Olivia reveals that she and Cesario are married. After the priest confirms the news, Orsino relents and denounces Cesario, saying they will never meet again.
- Sir Andrew and then Sir Toby enter, having both been injured fighting with Cesario, a charge Viola denies.
- Sir Toby rejects Sir Andrew's offer of help, calling him a 'gull'.
- Sebastian enters, apologising to Olivia for hurting her relative. He sees Antonio, who wonders which of the twins is Sebastian, and Viola and Sebastian are reunited.
- Orsino resolves to marry Viola and asks to see her in her own clothes. Viola reports that the Captain who has her garments is being held by Malvolio, which reminds Olivia of her benighted steward.
- Feste enters with Malvolio's letter which Fabian reads out.
- Malvolio arrives and he gives Olivia the counterfeit letter which Olivia recognises as Maria's handwriting.
- Fabian reveals the plot against Malvolio and that Sir Toby has married Maria for her part in it. Feste reminds Malvolio of his insults to him and Malvolio departs, swearing revenge on everyone.
- Alone, Feste sings a melancholic song and in its final lines addresses the audience.

ANALYSIS

HOW FINAL IS THE FINALE?

This finale, in a skilful mix of prose and **blank verse**, is a dazzling orchestration of the different strands of the plot, as almost all the players are brought together on stage and reveal their loves. The highly charged emotions of these serial revelations are expressed in frequent references to madness (carried over from Malvolio's scene in the darkened room in Act IV) and to witchcraft (for example, at line 65). As the play moves towards a kind of resolution, however, there are final twists: Olivia believes her new husband disdains her when Viola expresses her love, Orsino threatens to kill Cesario for his duplicity in marrying Olivia, and Malvolio promises revenge on the 'whole pack' (line 355). This last twist remains unresolved at the end of the play.

CHECK THE FILM **A03**

Some stage productions have chosen to accentuate the doubt surrounding the pairings of lovers by adding a comic moment in which Orsino initially approaches the wrong twin for his final proposal, while Trevor Nunn's 1996 film made several small changes to provide an ending that is reassuringly happy. In your view, which approach is more true to the spirit of the play and why?

Some critics have argued that the marriage based on a misapprehension is a punishment for Olivia's excessive behaviour at the opening of the play: a woman who refuses to be a part of 'normal' social and family life, preferring the love of a dead brother to that of an ardent new suitor, is disciplined by being made to humiliate herself in pursuit of a woman and then to marry a stranger. On the other hand, Olivia herself likens the rapidity of her love for Cesario to catching the 'plague' (I.5.250); she is lucky, perhaps, to escape from this dangerous condition with a suitable husband.

LOVE AND HATE

The flurry of declarations and revelations means that the long scene is structured around short and concentrated exchanges between the various true and false pairings, Olivia and Orsino, Olivia and Viola, Viola and Sebastian, Viola and Orsino, Sebastian and Antonio, with interruptions from Sir Toby, Sir Andrew, Feste and Malvolio. The spotlight of emotional intensity pinpoints different moments and combinations as all are brought to reveal their most passionate feelings of love. Orsino's love is close to hate, and is articulated primarily as a threat – 'Him I will tear out of that cruel eye' (line 116) – and in this he is close to the violence expressed by Malvolio and which comes from Antonio's description of his skirmishes with Orsino's forces.

STUDY FOCUS: MONEY A02

Orsino and Feste exchange some banter over money, which has been a constant concern through the play. The imaginative reality of Illyria is everywhere permeated with the everyday reality of money. From Viola's first words with the Captain, to here, coins frequently change hands and there are continual reminders of the need to pay bills and settle accounts. Sir Toby is heavily in debt to Sir Andrew, who, in his pursuit of Olivia, is considerably out of pocket. Sir Toby refuses to 'confine' himself, but money is the constraint which misrule cannot avoid. Malvolio's role as steward is to ensure economy and to balance the books. Feste is paid for his fooling and, as here, uses his wit to beg for money. Antonio lends Sebastian his purse. Notably Viola refuses money from Olivia, but Olivia will pay for the wedding celebrations to come. In a broader sense, however, all of the play's revelry takes place against the understanding voiced by Feste that 'pleasure will be paid, one time or another' (II.4.68), in other words, that pleasure in youth may be paid for with suffering in old age. Identify some of the many references to money in the play either in the dialogue or at work in the plot. What effect does the pervasive presence of money have on the festive antics and atmosphere of *Twelfth Night*? How does the idea of money relate to the title of the play?

LOVE'S LABOUR'S LOST?

After the twins are restored to each other, Orsino wants to see Viola in her 'woman's weeds' (line 257), and in the play's final **rhyming couplet**, before Feste's song, he reiterates that she will become his mistress when she is 'in other habits' (line 364). So the ending of *Twelfth Night* postpones the uniting of the lovers in marriage until a time beyond the end of the play. In *Love's Labour's Lost*, following the sudden news of the death of the Princess's father, the mood darkens and there is a similar delay to the lords' wooing of the ladies, in this case for a year and a day. In *Twelfth Night*, however, Viola twice states that her women's clothes are with the Captain (lines 239 and 259), whom, she also reveals, is being held by Malvolio 'upon some action' (line 259). So the precariousness of the happy ending is heightened since it is to some extent dependent on the alienated steward who has exited calling for revenge. It is important to recognise the way Shakespeare uses the suspended resolution in both comedies to create endings which mix light and dark elements and then to contrast it with the denouement in *As You Like It*, where Rosalind does appear in her 'woman's weeds'.

STUDY FOCUS: A HAPPY ENDING? A01

The play may seem to work towards a happy ending, in which not only lovers are united, but a brother is returned to Viola and Olivia gains Orsino as a brother. There are, however, those left out in the **metaphorical** cold. Sir Andrew has nothing to show for his expensive stay in Olivia's household; Antonio is soon forgotten when Sebastian is reunited with Viola; Feste is still singing his own mournful songs. Even the lovers may be thought to have been over-hastily paired off: Orsino's sudden proposal to his former page and Olivia's silent acceptance of her mystery husband suggest an ending that owes more to dramatic convention than to emotional truth. Director Michael Pennington notes that the final marriages 'have something perfunctory about them as if the fantastic contortions of the plot had made the characters into puppets'. We never see Viola back in her own clothes, although there are many references to them (see **Part Three: Themes**, on **Gender**), and so the homoerotic tinge of the relationship between Orsino and Cesario is daringly preserved, nor does she allow her brother to embrace her (line 235). The bitter-sweet mood of the play is encapsulated in the final scene's careful balance of feeling and choreography: *Twelfth Night*, as befits a play about the end of the festive season, has a melancholic edge to its final celebrations (see **Part Three: Themes**, on **Twelfth Night**).

CHECK THE PLAY A03

A variation on Feste's song, with its refrain 'the rain it raineth every day', is reprised in *King Lear*, when the Fool responds to Lear's words of pity. This time, however, the stanza is sung not at the end, but at the play's core, amid the rain of the raging storm on the heath. Compare the possible effect on the audience of Feste's final song with the Fool's version in *King Lear*.

KEY QUOTATION: ACT V SCENE 1 A02

Orsino: 'One face, one voice, one habit and two persons/ A natural perspective, that is and is not!' (lines 200–2)

- On seeing the identical twins both in male attire, Orsino declares that nature has created an optical illusion which is at once real and impossible.

- Orsino's statement balances the negative and positive, and affirms what the restoration of the twins reveals, that Viola and Sebastian, female and male, are not distinguishable by appearance.

- He describes their physical presence as a **paradox** of numbers, 'one' and yet 'two', and words, 'is and is not'.

- His phrase 'is and is not' recalls the many similar riddling variations on the the verb 'to be' in the play, such as Feste's opposite assertion as Sir Topas in the previous scene, 'That that is, is' (IV.2.13), or his earlier 'Nothing that is so, is so' (IV.1.6–7), or the many examples from Viola, which have blurred the boundaries between reality and illusion and questioned the nature of the self, so opening up possibilities of change and renewal in things and people.

GLOSSARY

16–17	**four negatives make your two affirmatives**	the jest suggests that no, no, no, no can be recalculated as yes, yes on the principle of the double negative becoming a positive
30	**the third pays for all**	third time lucky
42	**Vulcan**	in Roman mythology, smith to the gods
46	**bottom**	ship
50	**fraught**	cargo
	Candy	Candia, now Crete
54	**brabble**	brawl
60	**dear**	dire
68	**wrack**	person who has been shipwrecked
70	**retention**	reservation
77	**face me out**	deny to my face
78	**removèd thing**	stranger
80	**recommended**	committed
107	**th'Egyptian thief**	alluding to a popular story in which a brigand tried to kill his captive to prevent her being captured by his enemies
110	**non-regardance**	oblivion
114	**minion**	sexual favourite (disparaging term)
136	**strangle thy propriety**	deny your identity (as my husband)
154	**grizzle**	grey hairs
	case	fox skin
165	**coxcomb**	head
169	**incardinate**	Sir Andrew's mistake for 'incarnate' – in human form
177	**set nothing**	think nothing of
178	**halting**	limping
185	**passy-measures pavin**	a stately dance
188	**be dressed**	have our wounds dressed
221	**dimension**	physical form
	grossly	naturally
222	**participate**	have in common with others
233	**lets**	hinders
236	**cohere**	coincide
	jump	agree
239	**weeds**	clothes
255	**orbèd continent**	the sun
260	**durance**	imprisonment
264	**distract**	mentally disturbed
268	**Belzebub … end**	the devil at bay
271	**skills not**	doesn't matter
277	***vox***	the appropriate voice
280	**perpend**	pay attention
311	**from it**	differently
312	**invention**	composition
315	**lights**	signs, indications
325	**character**	handwriting
342	**importance**	importunity
345	**pluck on**	induce
348	**baffled**	disgraced
354	**whirligig**	spinning top
380	**tosspots**	drunkards

CHARACTERS

CHARACTERISATION

Characters in a play are just that: characters. It may seem obvious to say that they are not real people and that they should not be discussed as such. They consist of what they say and what is said about them: they are composed of words, not flesh and blood, and only have the inner psychology that the playwright allows them. It is significant that the very word 'character' derives from words denoting marking or writing (as in its use in *Twelfth Night* at V.1.344, when Olivia is describing the counterfeit handwriting in Malvolio's letter), and only gained its predominant modern meanings of 'individual personality' or 'person in a play' in the late seventeenth century.

Sometimes Shakespearean characters have a representative, rather than an individual function: they embody behaviours or characteristics as **symbolic** personifications. Sometimes naming can be a clue to this: the name 'Feste', for example, derives from the Latin *festivus* = a feast; the **etymology** and associations of Sir Toby Belch are rather cruder. Some characters exist as dramatic devices rather than as fully realised individuals – Fabian's role is plot-based, rather than psychological. At other times, Shakespeare's gift for recognisable and distinctive **characterisation** is evident: single phrases or gestures can suggest an entire personality, such as Sir Andrew Aguecheek's pensive 'I was adored once, too' (II.3.153).

In performance the assumptions of the **Method** school tend to dominate, whereby the inner motivations of the characters – their life beyond what is written for them in the play – are a crucial part of directors' and actors' interpretation. The following discussion uses information from modern performances where it offers a particular slant, but it also tries to remember that Shakespeare's characters derive from an age in which personality and the sense of the individual were quite different from now, and especially that they are part of a theatrical culture in which **verisimilitude** was not always the prime concern. When Fabian remarks knowingly that 'If this were played upon a stage now, I could condemn it as an improbable fiction' (III.4.108–9), he is revealing, rather than hiding, the artificiality of events (see **Part Five: Contexts and Critical Debates**, on **Historical Background**).

> **CRITICAL VIEWPOINT** **A03**
>
> Many critics have noted the central role of female characters in Shakespeare's comedies. Viola, like Rosalind in *As You Like It*, is an active heroine who takes the initiative. The other female characters in the play are also active and dominant. Olivia seizes her chance with Sebastian and Maria shows invention, wit and some venom as she becomes the prime mover in the plot against Malvolio, his transformed appearance according to her instructions being a comic highlight of the play.

VIOLA

WHO IS VIOLA?

- Viola is a young noblewoman, whose father died when she was thirteen.
- We first see her when she is cast up on the shore of Illyria, following a shipwreck in which her twin brother Sebastian has been lost.
- Amid her grief, she shows courage and resourcefulness in deciding to dress as a boy called Cesario and enter the service of Orsino.

VIOLA: SCHEMER OR CHARMER?

Throughout the play, Viola is a stranger in Illyria, a potentially inhospitable land. She appears as a woman only in her first scene and is not mentioned by her own name until the reunion with her twin brother in the final scene. In Act III Scene 4 she admits that she has consciously adopted Sebastian's appearance – in productions she often borrows his clothing from a chest saved from the wreck – and it may be that her disguise is a way of keeping her brother alive until their eventual reunion in Act V. Like Olivia (their names are virtual anagrams, signalling that they are made up of similar elements but in a different order), she has lost her father and, she fears, her brother; unlike Olivia, she does not respond to loss by retreating into herself, but gives herself up to the restorative powers of 'time' (II.2.37). Writing in the eighteenth century, Samuel Johnson described Viola as 'a cunning schemer, never at a loss'; the opposite view was taken by the critic William Hazlitt, who wrote in 1817 that she is 'the great and secret charm' of the play: 'much as we like cakes and ale there is something that we like better' (see **Part Five: Contexts and Critical Debates**).

STUDY FOCUS: VIOLA IN BETWEEN AND GO-BETWEEN · A02

Zoë Wanamaker, who played Viola at the Royal Shakespeare Theatre (1983–4), described her character as 'the catalyst of the play' who enters the 'locked-up stillness of Illyria' to bring 'life, and chaos, and hope', 'stirring up the place, forcing them all up into a spiral'. Viola is certainly associated with movement throughout the play: she is the go-between for Orsino to Olivia and moves between their households; she has individual conversations with Olivia, Orsino, Malvolio, Feste and Sebastian and, as such, is the major connective force between the different characters and plot strands. Her arrival breaks up the stalemate of Orsino's extravagant and unrequited love for Olivia, and equally dismantles the sterility of Olivia's self-imposed mourning. As Cesario she is able to challenge Orsino's glib sexism about women's inability to love, 'There is no woman's sides/ Can bide the beating of so strong a passion/ As love doth give my heart' (II.4.89–91), with her own heartfelt 'We men … prove/ Much in our vows, but little in our love' (II.4.112–14). She is also able to identify Olivia's pride (I.5.205), and thus reintroduce her to the world she has ignored. Find more examples of how Viola brings life to Illyria and Illyria to life.

STUDY FOCUS: VIOLA ALONE A02

For all her conversations – swapping witticisms with Feste, parrying Olivia's passionate questioning, at once evading and confessing to Orsino – Viola is in some sense alone for much of the play, unable to open up to anybody because of the disguise she calls 'a wickedness' (II.2.24). She has no confidante other than the audience, although the relative lack of **soliloquies** or **asides** addressed to the audience suggests that she does not really confide in us either. Her encounters with Orsino and Olivia are emotionally charged, but there is the constant echo of what must remain unspoken. Her love for Orsino is ventriloquised as the 'willow cabin' she would, were she he, build at Olivia's gate (I.5.223), or as the pining passion of her ill-fated imaginary sister who, like Viola herself, 'never told her love/ But let concealment, like a worm i'th'bud/ Feed on her damask cheek' (II.4.106–8). Her love can be voiced only in a kind of disguise, dressed as something or someone else, in an emotional and linguistic parallel to her physical disguise as Cesario.

VIOLA: 'I AM NOT THAT I PLAY'

Frequently Viola alludes to the disparity between her real self and the part she is playing: 'I am not that I play' (I.5.153), she tells Olivia at their first meeting. Helen Schlesinger, another RSC Viola, in 1997–8, found in her character an 'elusive' quality, describing it as 'a very lonely part. There's a bit of her that is always hidden', and this oblique aspect of Viola might be thought to remain even at the play's conclusion when the return of her woman's clothing keeps being referred to but never actually happens. Strikingly, for viewers of the play in the theatre (as opposed to readers of the text), she is not named as Viola and so does not attain the individual identity denoted by her forename until Sebastian greets her in Act V, 'Thrice welcome, drownèd Viola' (V.1.225). Then she speaks her own name twice in ten lines, the first time to talk about Viola and the second to make the decisive assertion of

the self, 'I am Viola' (line 237), but even then only in a long and complex sentence in which the statement is subordinate and heavily qualified. There is a sense, therefore, in which she cannot be a complete person until she is reunited in an embrace with her twin after the play's conclusion. Orsino, significantly, continues to call her 'Cesario' to the end. Perhaps, therefore the play's **symbolic** resolution is in the twins' embrace rather than in the final double marriages, which take place after the end of the play.

KEY QUOTATION: VIOLA A01

Viola: 'I am not what I am.' (III.1.126)

- Viola here uses one of the many riddling expressions concerning the verb 'to be' which occur through the play, to hint that her true self is secret and unknown.

- Viola's divided self is a condition she also identifies in Olivia, 'you do think you are not what you are' (III.1.124).

- When she is apparently closest to the man she loves, Viola's male disguise pushes her beyond reach, and yet this distance makes the woman who loves her want her all the more.

- This gap between self and identity is experienced by the other characters in *Twelfth Night* who all play parts and adopt roles which are not completely them.

CRITICAL VIEWPOINT A03

The shipwreck has **metaphorical** associations with the birth trauma separating the twins and therefore suggests that the whole play is an attempt to return to that privileged togetherness they enjoyed before birth. Stage productions sometimes make use of the same idea, such as the RSC production (1994) in which Emma Fielding as Viola describes 'emerging from billowing silk waves on to an empty shore, a rebirth I suppose and also the only time in the play when she is openly female and openly vulnerable.' (*Twelfth Night, Actors on Shakespeare*, 2002, p. 16.)

ORSINO

WHO IS ORSINO?

- Orsino is the Duke (or Count) of Illyria.
- The Captain tells Viola that Orsino is 'noble in nature as in name' (I.2.25).
- At the start of the play Orsino's professed love for Olivia is completely self-absorbed.
- Viola, as Cesario, offers him an understanding of the possibilities of female love, allowing him to move beyond his own ego to a love he finally describes as a 'combination … of dear souls' (V.1.360–1).

ORSINO THE ROMANTIC EGOIST

Orsino's famous declaration of love opens the play: 'If music be the food of love, play on' (I.1.1). He is immediately established as an extravagant lover, indulging his **hyperbolic** passion for a woman who has made it clear she does not want anything to do with him. His language is full of romance **clichés** and preoccupied with the exquisite masochism of unrequited love: 'my desires, like fell and cruel hounds/ E'er since pursue me' (I.1.22–3). He is more concerned with himself as lover than with the object of his love, suggesting he is narcissistic. In the opening scene he imagines that he will eventually be 'king' (I.1.39) of Olivia's affections, suggesting a marital hierarchy rather than mutuality.

STUDY FOCUS: ORSINO AND CESARIO | **A02**

Viola, as Cesario, in telling the story of her 'sister', wrests Orsino's attention from his self-indulgent protestations (see **Extended Commentary: Act II Scene 4 lines 83–120**). From this emotional scene in which she disguises her love for him and plants the suggestion that his view of women is inadequate and restricted, he does not appear again until the end of the play. By this time, his emotional reliance on Cesario has eclipsed his love for Olivia, so that when he mistakenly believes they are married, his sense of betrayal falls not on his worshipped mistress but on his 'page': 'this your minion, whom I know you love,/ And whom, by heaven I swear, I tender dearly,/ Him will I tear out of that cruel eye/ Where he sits crownèd in his master's spite' (V.1.114–17). The proposed marriage between Cesario and Olivia shocks Orsino into a declaration of love for 'Cesario': 'I'll sacrifice the lamb that I do love' (V.1.119).

Through Viola's disguise, she and Orsino have got to know each other before recognising each other as lovers. Orsino responds quickly and openly to the newcomer: 'Thou knowest no less but all: I have unclasped/ To thee the book even of my secret soul' (I.4.12–13). There is, however, a lingering sense that it was the boy Cesario with whom Orsino fell in love, and his final words to his bride stress the homoerotic foundations of their relationship: 'Cesario, come –/ For so you shall be while you are a man' (V.1.362–3). Their relationship, therefore, contributes to the sexually ambiguous undertones of the play's many depictions of love (see **Part Three: Themes**, on **Love and self-love**, and **Part Five: Critical Debates**). Analyse in detail how Cesario leads Orsino out of his romantic bondage to Olivia to a bond of mutual love with Viola.

KEY QUOTATION: ORSINO | **A01**

Orsino: 'But died thy sister of her love, my boy?' (II.4.115)

- With this question, Orsino moves beyond his egotistical and mysogynistic outburst at the start of the scene to an awareness, through Cesario, of love in another.
- The diction (monosyllables) and sound (near rhymes 'died thy', 'sister of her love', 'my boy') heighten the tender and naive quality of the Duke's enquiry.
- The contrast between his previous anger and his subsequent concern makes the Duke's question even more poignant.

OLIVIA

WHO IS OLIVIA?

- Olivia is a beautiful countess whose father died a year previously and brother died soon afterwards.
- The Captain describes her as 'A virtuous maid' (I.2.36).
- She resolves to remain in mourning and shun society for seven years.
- When she meets Cesario she yields herself up to her love for him and so moves beyond her grief, her desire being finally deflected into a marriage with Viola's twin brother Sebastian.

LIFTING THE VEIL ON OLIVIA

We hear a good deal about Olivia before she appears on stage: Orsino, the Captain, Sir Toby, Sir Andrew, Maria and Feste all mention her before her first entrance in Act I Scene 5. This extended introduction is entirely suitable for a character who is the focus of the idealising love of Orsino and Sir Andrew, neither of whom ever speaks directly to her until the last scene, the self-serving ambitions of Malvolio, the freeloading of Sir Toby, and the **satiric** wit of Feste. Each of these characters has a different idea of what lies behind her veil of mourning. The veil is an appropriate **symbol**: perhaps we never really know what motivates this woman who first rejects the world and love and then quickly falls for a young page who comes to visit her.

STUDY FOCUS: OLIVIA'S MARRIAGE — A02

Olivia's urgent desire for Cesario leads her to a hasty marriage with Sebastian, but following her new husband's revelation that she is 'betrothed both to a maid and man' (V.1.247) she does not respond. How should we read her silence? She fell in love with Viola's words to her, not simply with Cesario's appearance. The first aspect she praised on Cesario's departure was his 'tongue' (I.5.247), so it is not clear whether the outward similarity between her desired and her actual partner will be enough: essentially, she marries a man who looks exactly like a woman she fell in love with, which may not be an altogether happy start for a marriage. With reference to Olivia's words and actions through the play, analyse the case for and against her marriage to Sebastian as a happy outcome for the Countess. How do you think we should interpret her lack of response to the revelation about her husband at the end of the play?

KEY QUOTATION: OLIVIA — A01

Olivia: 'Stay!/ I prithee tell me what thou think'st of me.' (III.1.122–3)

- A simple monosyllable takes up a whole line, emphasising that there should be a pause here to underline the dramatic force of the imperative.
- Olivia shifts from commanding to begging, as she tries to evoke an open response from the page, her earlier more tentative 'What might you think?' (III.1.102) becoming a direct and intimate appeal.
- She uses the familiar 'thee' to reduce the formal distance between them.
- Her simple question prompts the response from Viola that Olivia does not truly know her own self.

CHECK THE PLAY — A03

Orsino and Olivia both refer to the attractiveness of Cesario's lips. Orsino says, 'Diana's lip/ Is not more smooth and rubious' (I.5.30–1); and Olivia, 'O what a deal of scorn looks beautiful/ In the contempt and anger of his lip' (III.1.130–1). In Olivia's case her own lips are the first item listed in her parody of a **blazon**, '*item*, two lips, indifferent red…' (1.5.202). So the text perhaps gives some justification for the trend in modern stage productions for kisses on the lips between characters in *Twelfth Night*, for instance when Olivia declares her love for Cesario.

MALVOLIO

WHO IS MALVOLIO?

- Malvolio is the steward in the Countess Olivia's household, a highly responsible position which places him in charge of accounts, staff and practical matters.
- He is called a 'a kind of puritan' (II.3.119) by Maria, but she makes clear she is talking generally about his strait-laced attitude rather than his membership of the Protestant sect.
- On his first appearance, the Countess notes that he is 'sick of self-love' (I.5.73) and it is his inability to move beyond his narcissism which leads to his gulling, imprisonment and final exit swearing revenge.

MALVOLIO: A COMPLEX CHARACTER

John Manningham's account of an early performance of *Twelfth Night* takes particular delight in the Malvolio plot (see **Part One: Introducing *Twelfth Night***, on ***Twelfth Night* in Context**), and this enjoyment has been an ongoing feature in audience responses to the play on the stage. The spectacle of the gullible, aspiring, hypocritical steward made to look a fool by those he has humiliated seems to appeal, both on- and off-stage. There are, however, two ways to look at Malvolio's entry in Act II Scene 3. An unsympathetic interpretation would see Malvolio as the voice of the self-righteous when faced with revellers, a man who enjoys his moral superiority over his social superiors. According to this reading, Malvolio's own pomposity sets him up for his humiliation, and the speed with which he is persuaded that Olivia loves him shows his social-climbing self-delusion. If Malvolio is seen in a more positive light, however, we might think that he is only doing his job as the conscientious steward of a household that is still in mourning and in which, therefore, loud revelry is most inappropriate. In this light it is Sir Toby and the others who are in the wrong, and Malvolio is the victim of his own diligence. There is some support for this second view in Olivia's concern for her seemingly mad steward: 'I would not have him miscarry for the half of my dowry' (III.4.56–7). Clearly she relies on Malvolio to manage her household.

CHECK THE FILM A03

In Trevor Nunn's 1996 film Malvolio is shown in his room alone reading a salacious French magazine *Amour*, a detail which suggests his hypocrisy, but in the 1981 BBC TV production, Malvolio is portrayed as deluded, but sincere. With reference to the text, decide which interpretation is more valid in your view.

STUDY FOCUS: IS MALVOLIO A HYPOCRITE? A02

Many productions have attempted to suggest that Malvolio is a hypocrite. In Act II Scene 5 (lines 41–55) the alacrity and clarity with which he imagines himself husband to Olivia show that he is not so puritanical as he might seem: his mind tends towards fantasies of sex ('having come from a day-bed, where I have left Olivia sleeping'), material possessions ('wind up my watch or play with my – some rich jewel') and power ('I extend my hand to him thus – quenching my familiar smile with an austere regard of control'). The preposterous vision of his acting out these fantasies in the orchard establishes him as an inflated individual who needs to be taken down a notch. Having said that, however, we may well feel that the joke against him goes too far (see **Part Three: Themes**, on **Twelfth Night**).

MALVOLIO PUNISHED

Certainly Malvolio is thoroughly punished. While he is not alone in 'self-love' (I.5.73) – this is a feature of the behaviour of Orsino and Olivia too – he is disciplined and humiliated for this failing, rather than, as they are, educated out of it through love. He is not alone in aspiring to an apparently unreachable love object either: Viola, Olivia, Antonio and Orsino all do this to some degree, and Maria, another household employee, eventually does marry far above her social station. The extent of Malvolio's punishment, then, makes him seem like a scapegoat, bearing the displaced penalty of the failings of the whole cast. His role suggests the cruelty inherent in comedy: the sour taste left after 'what you will' (See **Part Three: Themes**, on **Twelfth Night**).

Michael Bogdanov (who co-founded the English Shakespeare Company with Michael Pennington) in his Ludlow production (2004) went to the extreme in upsetting the comic balance by making Malvolio exit in silence at the revelation of his gulling, then allowing the comic denouement to unfold before finally having Malvolio return with troops to tear down the festive decorations and issue his threat as the last words of the play! Malvolio is sometimes seen to become a tragic figure at the end, but *Twelfth Night* is a comedy. Consider why people might sometimes view him as tragic. Why can he never attain the status of true tragic characters such as Hamlet or King Lear?

KEY QUOTATION: MALVOLIO   A01

Malvolio: 'I'll be revenged on the whole pack of you!' (V.1.355)

- Malvolio's last words are an explicit and discordant threat, among the marriages, explanations and reconciliations that characterise the final scene.

- Malvolio rejects Olivia's gracious sympathy and Fabian's assertion that the 'sportful malice … May rather pluck on laughter than revenge' (V.1.344–5).

- He fails to acquire the 'generous, guiltless … free disposition' (I.5.74–5) which from the outset Olivia suggests he lacks.

- Malvolio extends his implacable hostility to Feste and his tormentors to all the company, his threat of revenge upsetting the play's comic resolution.

- His pompous mentality and unflinching rectitude are hostile to the spirit of the play which has 'foolery' at its heart, and so Malvolio places himself beyond redemption and exits the comedy.

REVISION FOCUS: TASK 3   A02

How far do you agree with the following statements?

- The overwhelming evidence of the play points towards Malvolio being an essentially tragic, rather than comic figure.

- The most memorable dramatic moments of the play feature Malvolio. Without him the play's dramatic impact would be considerably lessened.

Try writing opening paragraphs for essays based on these discussion points. Set out your arguments clearly.

FESTE

WHO IS FESTE?

- Feste is the professional fool in Olivia's household, but, after an absence, his position is insecure.

- Feste is a musician whose songs act on both characters and audience to help to create the peculiar mixture of merriness and melancholy in the play.

- His need to use his wits to beg for money is a constant reminder of hard economic realities which threaten to impinge on the revelry in Illyria.

- Feste's role as an 'allowed fool' (I.5.76) gives him the freedom to speak his own wry and enigmatic form of wisdom, his 'foolosophy'.

FESTE THE COMMENTATOR

Perhaps Feste is less a character than a function. He has a **choric**, commentary role, rather than a participatory one. His strength comes from his observation: 'He must observe their mood on whom he jests,/ ... This is a practice/ As full of labour as a wise man's art' (Viola, III.1.52–6). Perhaps, as Cesario suggests in Act III Scene 1, he knows more than he is letting on. He may be an older man: having been fool to Olivia's father, he provides a link with her family history which has been fractured by the recent deaths of her father and brother.

FESTE'S WISDOM

Feste embodies the disinterested clarity denied to the other characters who are too wrapped up in the unfolding plot. As Viola observes, 'This fellow is wise enough to play the fool' (III.1.50). His role is to point out the truths other characters do not want to hear: the grief-stricken Olivia that her brother is in heaven and therefore beyond mourning; the carousing Sir Toby that he lies when he speaks of his own immortality (II.3.91); Orsino, who is boasting male constancy, that he is as changeable as the opal (II.4.71); Cesario that he wants a beard (III.1.38). His is a wit that is always tinged with melancholy: his songs reverberate with ageing, death and with winter weather. It is not surprising that the song with which he ends the play crops up again in Shakespeare's bleakest tragedy, *King Lear*.

 CHECK THE PLAY **A03**

In the 'original practice' revival of the 2012 Globe production the precariousness of Feste's position was emphasised in his first exchange with Olivia. The Countess peremptorily dismissed Peter Hamilton Dyer's Feste and busied herself in paperwork while he was being dragged offstage for good. He had to use his quick wits to try to capture her attention in order to retrieve his position, giving a vital energy and purpose to his jesting.

CHECK THE PLAY **A03**

Productions often emphasise Feste's position as observer. At the RSC in 1979, Feste remained on stage throughout the play, cueing characters' entrances like a kind of stage-manager. Trevor Nunn's 1996 film had Feste, played by Ben Kingsley, watching from the clifftop as Viola made her way up the beach, showing that he alone sees through Cesario's disguise.

FESTE AND THE ENDING

Feste has a unique position in the play's structure. He participates in the action and through his music he affects the mood and atmosphere, but he also stands apart as an observer of characters and events and provides a commentary in a choric role. It is fitting, therefore, that the play ends with Feste's song, which is the bridge to leave the time and imaginary possibilities of the world of Illyria, for the time and the realities of the everyday world of the audience.

STUDY FOCUS: FESTE AND MALVOLIO — A02

Feste drops his disengaged stance in the baiting of Malvolio. As their names suggest (Feste = feast, festivity and Malvolio = ill-will) the two represent opposed polarities: the anarchic and the methodical; the irreverent and the sycophantic; the spender and the hoarder. They are also placed at opposite ends in their attitude to language: Feste fools with words, but is not fooled by them; to be taken in by words, fixing them with a narrow sense, is Malvolio's error. Perhaps Malvolio touches a nerve in his acidic observation at their first encounter in the play: 'Unless you laugh and minister occasion to him, he is gagged' (I.5.70–1); to the verbal juggler such a fate would be terrible. Feste refers again to it in the final scene, so the insult has not been forgotten: 'and you smile not, he's gagged' (line 353). Like any professional comedian, Feste needs the approval of an audience: without that, he is as good as gagged. Malvolio's refusal to play along is the source of Feste's opposition to him. We see the fool's disinterest turn to cruelty in his disguise as Sir Topas, but as Feste he provides Malvolio with pen, ink and paper, through which words will become the steward's means to freedom. Analyse the contrasts between Feste and Malvolio to explain how their characters work as polar opposites in the play.

GRADE BOOSTER — A01

Stephen Boxer, who played Feste for the RSC in 1997–8, described the importance of language to Feste: 'Some of the more obscure meanings you can make clear by vocal tricks and gesture. He creates his own language – not necessarily sense in the way that other characters speak but an anarchic kind of sense.' Analyse Feste's wordplay to show how he creates apparent nonsense to make a deeper kind of sense.

KEY QUOTATION: FESTE — A01

Feste: 'I am indeed not her fool but her corrupter of words.' (III.1.29–30)

- It is through his verbal dexterity that Feste expresses his own oblique perspective on the events of the play.

- He manipulates language through **puns**, sayings, jokes and catechising to reveal the folly of other characters, such as in his first scene with Olivia, where, responding to her exasperated 'Take the fool away', he replies, 'Do you not hear, fellows? Take away the lady' (I.5.31–2).

  - Through his fooling with words and also in his songs, he frees language to become a source of intellectual, emotional and physical pleasure.

  - His wordplay demonstrates that language itself is slippery and not to be fully trusted: 'Truth, sir, I can you none [no reason] without words, and words are grown so false, I am loath to prove reason with them' (III.1.20–1).

SIR TOBY

WHO IS SIR TOBY?

- Sir Toby is related, or as he puts it 'consanguineous' (II.3.67), to Olivia.
- The Countess is referred to as his 'niece', though his precise relationship is not clear, she referring to him by the more general 'cousin'.
- His name suggests over-indulgence, and in most of his scenes he is drinking or drunk.
- While relying on Olivia's goodwill to stay in her household, he exploits his friend Sir Andrew Aguecheek by encouraging him to woo the Countess.
- Following the plot against Malvolio, he marries Maria, Olivia's gentlewoman.

REVELRY'S DARKER SIDE

It has been suggested that in the **characterisation** of Sir Toby Belch, Shakespeare was trying to recreate his most successful comic conception, the fat and disreputable knight of the *Henry IV* plays, Falstaff. However, perhaps the jollity is all a case of over-compensation for a man who has lost a nephew (Olivia's dead brother) and, like Olivia and Viola, a brother in Olivia's father. Sometimes Sir Toby has been played as a man having one last fling before settling into a more respectable old age; hence, perhaps, Feste's pointed references to time passing in the drinking scene. Seen in this light, his marriage to Maria is part of the 'last chance' mood (see **Part Three: Themes**, on **Twelfth Night**).

STUDY FOCUS: SIR TOBY, FREE SPIRIT OR FREELOADER? **A02**

Is Sir Toby a plump and genial *bon viveur*, the embodiment of the **carnival** spirit of excess and self-gratification, or is he a freeloader, 'sponging off' his niece and off his companion Sir Andrew? As with Malvolio, his opposite, there are many ways to see his character but, unlike Malvolio, audiences have generally been sympathetic to this profligate, humorous and self-indulgent rogue described by director Michael Pennington as 'deadly fun, completely without morals, articulate, witty and full-blooded'.

Yet Sir Toby shows little regard for any other character. His first words criticise Olivia for her mourning, and his last ones disparage Sir Andrew. There are flashes of friction between him and Feste. His wooing of Maria is a largely off-stage business, and his admiration is linked firmly with her plotting against Malvolio. His habitually elevated diction – words such as 'cubiculo' (III.2.41) and 'encounter' (III.1.64) – suggests a man of learning but also one with an **ironic**, self-conscious approach to proceedings. His motivations are sometimes difficult to discern: in the matter of the duel between Sir Andrew and Cesario, for example, he seems merely to enjoy the spectacle of these reluctant swordsmen. Is the audience's affection for Sir Toby warranted? Explain your views with close reference to his words and actions.

KEY QUOTATION: SIR TOBY **A01**

Sir Toby: 'Confine? I'll confine myself no finer than I am …' (I.3.8)

- Confinement, modesty and order are antipathetic to Toby's excessive and disorderly conduct (See **Part Three: Themes**, on **Twelfth Night** and **Excess**).
- His excess is also evident in his garrulous nature and an extravagance with language in which words are not completely in his control.
- He even rejects the authority of clock-time and perhaps, by extension, the limitation of time itself.
- His swaggering excesses are punished at the end, however, with a stark reminder of the limits of the body, when he receives a wound from Sebastian, leaving him ironically to berate drunkenness.

GRADE BOOSTER **A02**

The particular tension between Malvolio and Sir Toby arises not simply from their opposing temperaments, but because of the differing nature of their positions in Olivia's household, one based on kinship and the other derived from a powerful role. Following Sir Toby's contempt during the late-night drinking, Malvolio fantasises about marrying Olivia in order that he may be in a position to rule over Sir Toby. With reference to their characters and social status, analyse the antagonism between Sir Toby and Malvolio. Why is their animosity so intense?

SIR ANDREW

WHO IS SIR ANDREW?

- Sir Andrew Aguecheek is a wealthy companion of Sir Toby.
- He is slow-witted, cowardly and quarrelsome, with seemingly no voice and opinions of his own, but his presence is the basis for much of the play's action.
- Sir Toby encourages him to be a suitor to the Countess Olivia to indulge himself at Sir Andrew's expense.
- The practice of Sir Andrew being fooled for money, or 'gulled', started before the events of the play and continues to the final scene when Sir Toby reveals it in his final vicious outburst (V.1.190–1).

STUDY FOCUS: SIR ANDREW, MORE THAN A SHADOW — A02

Sir Andrew's 'gulling' is not in the forefront of the action, but without the late-night singing there would have been no plot against Malvolio and he also crosses into the main plot to duel with Cesario and bring Viola close to revealing her disguise. Sir Andrew's role in the last twenty-five or so lines of Act II Scene 5 **symbolises** his role throughout the play. Here his words echo those of his robust companion Sir Toby. Sir Andrew also shadows Orsino: his comically unrequited wooing of Olivia – the two are never on stage at the same time until after Olivia's marriage – is a fainter version of Orsino's passion. When Andrew and Cesario are at the point of duelling, the spectacle is of two unmanly opponents: the effeminate Sir Andrew and the disguised Viola. Sir Andrew is repeatedly characterised as a fool who does not understand French, who misunderstands words and uses them wrongly (as at I.3.45–6), who must borrow wooing terms from a page (III.1.76–7), and whose masculinity is in question (Maria's **pun** on 'dry' suggests impotence at I.3.60). Often he is shown unwittingly wearing yellow until he learns it is Olivia's least favourite colour. There is a hint of **pathos**, however, a past life lost, in his wistful words 'I was adored once, too' (II.3.153) and in the severity of Sir Toby's rejection of his help at the end. Consider Sir Andrew Aguecheek and his role in the play. Show how Shakespeare combines comedy and pathos to create an affecting comic character who is linked to much of the play's action.

CHECK THE PLAY — A03

Sir Andrew can be usefully considered in relation to another ineffectual wooer, Slender, in *The Merry Wives of Windsor*. Such a comparison reveals that, unlike Slender, Sir Andrew has an individuality which exceeds his function in the play. Compare and contrast the two wooers to highlight the different facets of Sir Andrew's character.

KEY QUOTATION: SIR ANDREW — A01

Sir Andrew: 'I knew 'twas I, for many do call me fool.' (II.5.67)

- Sir Andrew is deceived, but he has moments, as here, when he refers to his limitations in wit and as a wooer (see I.3.70–1 and I.3.86–7).
- These moments place him above the seemingly more intelligent Malvolio, whose vanity already deceives him into thinking he has real prospects with Olivia before he ever reads Maria's letter.
- They also help to engender sympathy and engagement for a figure who might otherwise be merely an object of ridicule.

SEBASTIAN

WHO IS SEBASTIAN?

- Sebastian is Viola's twin brother, 'both born in an hour' (II.1.13–14).
- Sebastian looks like Viola, or, more precisely, he is identical to Cesario.
- The arrival of Sebastian reassures the audience that the resolution to the dilemmas created by Viola's disguise, involving Orsino, Olivia and also Sir Andrew, will be benign.

SEBASTIAN: UNTYING THE KNOTS

Since Sebastian's major purpose is to be like someone else, it is perhaps not surprising that he could be seen to have little strength of personality himself. He is a virtual cipher, a plot function, a way of untying the knots into which the play has tangled itself. Although he attracts strong feelings from a sister who believes he is dead, from a seaman who saved him from the ocean and will sacrifice anything for him, from a woman who marries him as soon as she sees him, in his own person he is rather insignificant, appearing in only four scenes. His first entrance shows him bemoaning 'the malignancy of my fate' (II.1.3), mourning his sister 'with salt water' (line 22); he seems hardly to notice the doglike devotion of Antonio. In his second scene, he expresses his gratitude for Antonio's company, and proposes, perhaps rather immaturely, that they do some sightseeing. His questions of Antonio about the precise nature of his offence against Orsino's sailors might also reveal a kind of youthful inexperience. Sebastian is performing his own deeds of derring-do in his next scene, the fight with Sir Andrew when he is mistaken for Cesario. Here he meets Olivia, and is entranced by her kindness to him, believing himself asleep but agreeing to be 'ruled' by her (IV.1.57).

STUDY FOCUS: THE REUNION 〔A02〕

Sebastian's entrance into the final scene of the play is as 'the very devil incarnate' (V.1.169) who has wounded Sir Toby and Sir Andrew. He greets Antonio warmly: 'How have the hours racked and tortured me,/ Since I have lost thee!' (lines 203–4). His reunion with Viola is slower, more halting in their mutual rediscovery. His last words to Olivia are the rueful 'You are betrothed both to a maid and man' (line 247): there is no further conversation between or about them which would give any clue about how she has taken this news. Sebastian's insubstantiality is an inevitable function of his role in the plot. Analyse the reunion between Viola and Sebastian and its effect on the other characters. How does Shakespeare make the restoration of the twins so moving for the audience?

KEY QUOTATION: SEBASTIAN 〔A01〕

Sebastian: 'A spirit I am indeed/ But am in that dimension grossly clad/ Which from the womb I did participate.' (V.1.220–2)

- In response to Viola's fear that he is a spirit posing as her twin brother, Sebastian acknowledges that he is a spirit, but in a body.
- While providing in Sebastian a physical solution to the plot dilemmas and problems of desire which have unfolded between the characters, Shakespeare stresses the miraculous aspects of the reunion between the twins.
- This tone of spiritual union in the denouement culminates in Orsino's final words as he evokes a 'solemn combination ... Of our dear souls' (V.1.360–1).

GRADE BOOSTER 〔A02〕

In writing about Sebastian you will need to interrogate his actions and words very closely to get a sense of his 'character'; you could focus on his willingness to submit to the 'madness' of Olivia's love for him and contrast that with the manner in which his sister has to suppress similar feelings. But, is there an argument that Sebastian is emasculated by the passive role he plays in response to Olivia's, and Antonio's, love for him?

ANTONIO

WHO IS ANTONIO?

- Antonio is a sea captain who rescues Sebastian 'from the breach of the sea' after the shipwreck (II.1.16).
- He is a wanted man in Illyria after he engaged in a 'sea-fight' (III.3.26) with ships of Count Orsino.
- Despite the danger he faces in Illyria, he follows Sebastian and lends him his purse.
- He is arrested defending the disguised Viola, whom he believes to be Sebastian, in the duel with Sir Andrew.
- Alone of all the characters in the play, Antonio knows whom he loves, articulates that love, and acts selflessly because of it.

ANTONIO: SELFLESS DEVOTION

Antonio's actions are all prompted by his affection for Sebastian, expressed in the brief **soliloquy**: 'I do adore thee so' (II.1.35). It is striking, therefore, that he remains outside the charmed circle of couples at the end of the play: once Sebastian has been reunited with Viola he spares not a word for his protector, who is almost forgotten in the general celebrations and explanations.

STUDY FOCUS: ANTONIO'S LOVE   A02

Many productions have chosen to suggest that Antonio's love is not platonic but sexual, and certainly the vehemence of his feelings gives strength to this interpretation. This hint of homoeroticism combines with the ambiguous sexuality of Orsino's intimacy with his page Cesario and Olivia's love for Viola-disguised-as-Cesario (see **Part Five: Contexts and Critical Debates**). Whether or not Antonio is homosexual (the term itself did not exist in the Elizabethan period), his is a role **characterised** by self-sacrificing love for a man who seems scarcely to register, let alone earn, this devotion.

KEY QUOTATION: ANTONIO   A01

Antonio: 'This youth … to his image, which methought did promise/ Most venerable worth, did I devotion.' (III.4.310–14)

- Antonio expresses his love for Sebastian with a religious intensity.
- His pain and rage are deepened by his disappointment as an older man apparently betrayed by a youth.
- Shakespeare explores with a similar sacred fervour the love of an older for a younger man in his **sonnets**.

CRITICAL VIEWPOINT A03

In *The Fruits of the Sport* (1960), Bertrand Evans writes: 'Shakespeare has balanced our awareness between laughter and pain. These contradictory impulses, equal in power, stimulated by complex awareness, do not cancel each other out, leaving indifference; they battle for supremacy, and the intensity of their struggle determines the degree of our involvement.'

THEMES

TWELFTH NIGHT, OR WHAT YOU WILL

DOUBLES

The play is unique among Shakespeare's best-known works in having a double title, and this might be seen to introduce the theme of doubling or duplication from the outset – a theme that has other expressions in the two households of Orsino and Olivia, the **motif** of the twins, and the relationship between the almost anagrammatical Olivia and Viola, each of whom mourns a dead brother and father.

TWELFTH NIGHT

The play's first title, *Twelfth Night*, refers to the feast of the Epiphany on 6 January, the final day of the Christmas festivities. Since there is no explicit reference to this time of year within the play, scholars have argued, following Leslie Hotson's *The First Night of Twelfth Night* (1954), that it was first performed on this occasion in 1601. This is neat, but unsubstantiated: there is no real evidence that the play was first performed, or written, for the Twelfth Night celebrations. The play has an unreal quality of pretence: it is full of unlikely coincidences and interrelations appropriate to a time when normal rules and behaviours are suspended. The play does mention other festivals, although not Twelfth Night itself: Olivia judges Malvolio's behaviour 'midsummer madness' (III.4.50) and Fabian talks about the farcical duel preparations of Sir Andrew and Cesario as 'More matter for a May morning' (III.4.120).

CAKES AND ALE

Eating and drinking are a major part of the plot with Sir Toby the outlandish 'Lord of Misrule' in Olivia's household (see **Themes**, on **Excess**). If Act II Scene 3 with Sir Toby and Sir Andrew carousing into the night represents the spirit of festival or **carnival**, then Malvolio is an anti-festival figure, a killjoy, whose punishment, being imprisoned in a dark room, ultimately defends the right to enjoy 'cakes and ale' (II.3.99) and is the ultimate and terrifying experience of endless winter.

STUDY FOCUS: OR WHAT YOU WILL A01

If 'Twelfth Night' suggests festivity, but more insistently the end of festivity with the associations of winter and old age, the play's subtitle, 'What You Will', gives a different slant to interpretations of the play. Shakespeare enjoyed **punning** on the word 'will', including on his own name, particularly in his **sonnets**, and the phrase here could be paraphrased in a number of ways: what you want, what you would like, what you desire, what you please, whatever you want, over to you, have it your way, so you say, anything goes. Any of these could be applied to the play's characters, who 'will' themselves into new identities and new possibilities: Viola as Cesario, Olivia as a wife, Orsino out of masochistic love, Malvolio as Count, Sir Andrew as a fierce dueller. The phrase also poses a challenge to us as readers or audience: we can do what we want with the play, it's up to us. We have to take some responsibility. Our laughter supported the initial 'gulling' of Malvolio, but perhaps things did go too far. Like the cautionary fairy tales which warn how problematic it is to have our wishes granted, the play suggests that what we 'will' may not always turn out to be what we thought or really want, and so it simultaneously questions and indulges some of our fantasies.

ONE LAST COMEDY

While *Twelfth Night* has a sense of its own revels ending, it also forms an ending of Shakespeare's own period of writing romantic comedy. During the 1590s romantic comedy ending in marriage and harmony was a major part of Shakespeare's repertoire, whereas the first decade of the seventeenth century was to be characterised by an intense focus on tragedy (see **Part Five: Contexts and Critical Debates**, on **Historical Background**). Even Malvolio's parting words of revenge (V.1.355) look forward to another kind of play with an altogether different mood – the tragedies on which Shakespeare was to concentrate for the next decade. Perhaps this sense of *Twelfth Night* as his last comedy also adds a note of wistfulness to the revels. Put this way, it seems that it is Malvolio who has ultimately triumphed at the end, despite his personal humiliation.

STUDY FOCUS: THE END OF FESTIVITIES   A02

Twelfth Night is not only a festival, but a culmination of the days of merrymaking marking Christmas. It represents the end of things. It is the last day of feasting and merriment before normal life, self-denial, winter darkness and the old regulations set in. It is the day when the Christmas decorations come down and the house suddenly looks bare. Shakespeare's play picks up the elegiac, wistful associations of the end of the festival period. There is a sense of the clock ticking, of a limit to the festival world, of normal life waiting in the wings, even a sense of urgency about the revelry. The play closes not on the image of the two newly formed couples but on Feste, the distinctly unfestive clown. Feste's final song stresses that 'the rain it raineth every day' (V.1.389): the realities of winter weather cannot be shut out of the party. The play ends with a song of resolution which brings melancholy but also humour, since the repeated refrain is an example of comic exaggeration. The play's references to cold, such as the image of the unrequited lover 'hang[ing] like an icicle on a Dutchman's beard' (III.2.21–2), cannot be entirely banished by the warm glow of its romantic ending. If the play has provided its audience with an umbrella against this intemperate climate, it is clearly stated as a loan and so the respite, like the midwinter festival itself, is only temporary. Nevertheless, the song ends with the promise that the effort to raise the umbrella once more will go on.

CHECK THE PLAY   A03

The RSC director Terry Hands took the end of revelry as the keynote of his 1979 production: 'the festive moment has passed, and this is now the cruellest point of the year'. He saw Act II Scene 3 as the wretched attempt of the revellers to recapture the spirit of the festival, trying 'to put their Christmas tree back up'.

KEY QUOTATION: TWELFTH NIGHT   A01

Olivia: 'The clock upbraids me with the waste of time.' (III.1.115)

- The sense of the festivities coming to a close in *Twelfth Night* can be traced through the play's references to time.

- Here the striking clock changes Olivia's attitude to Cesario, perhaps referring not only to the current interview but to the length of her mourning and the sense of time passing and lost for ever (see **Extended Commentary: Act III Scene 1 lines 96–149**).

- There is also a sense of hurry, even a desperation, about Olivia's marriage to Sebastian, which she acknowledges but does not explain in saying, 'Blame not this haste of mine' (IV.3.22); she seems to need to seize the moment since it might never recur.

- Sir Toby's attempt in Act II Scene 3 to defy the clock and extend the party through the night also has an air of impotent rebellion about it, skewered neatly by Feste's unflinching song: 'Youth's a stuff will not endure' (line 46) and his reply to Sir Toby's 'But I will never die': 'Sir Toby, there you lie' (lines 90–1).

- Old age and its symbolic counterpart, winter, are never far beneath the surface in *Twelfth Night* and Feste's final song takes different perspectives on the passage of time before releasing the audience back into the every day.

EXCESS

APPETITES AND PASSIONS

Related to the theme of Twelfth Night is the theme of excess, which is not only a matter of eating and drinking in the play. From Orsino's desire for 'excess' of music (I.1.2) to the arguably excessive length of Olivia's mourning, from Malvolio 'sick' of excessive self-love (I.5.73) to the 'extravagancy' of Sebastian's voyage (II.1.7), the play is preoccupied with immoderate passions.

STUDY FOCUS: THE 'LIMITS OF ORDER'   A02

These excesses are, for the most part, moderated or brought into line by the end of the play. Orsino is educated about the real nature of women by his conversations with Cesario and into a love based on the intimacy of companionship rather than idealisation from afar. Olivia is jolted out of her sterile dependence on her dead male relatives into sudden passionate love. Malvolio is humiliated for his vain ambition and his presumption in believing Olivia is in love with him. It seems that the play endorses Maria's suggestion to Sir Toby, that he 'confine [himself] within the modest limits of order' (I.3.6–7), as immoderate desire is regulated by the triple marriages with which *Twelfth Night* concludes.

LOVE AND SELF-LOVE

ORSINO, CESARIO AND VIOLA

Comedies are generally about courtship leading to marriage, but *Twelfth Night* shows a number of variations on the theme of love, particularly around the difference between selfish and selfless love. Orsino's initial passion for Olivia seems based more on an idea of himself as a lover than on an acknowledgement of her separateness as a loved one. In turning from Olivia to Viola in the final scene, he shows how he has been educated out of narcissistic infatuation and into a relationship based on mutual intimacy. Another reading of this final marriage, however, would stress that the apparent intimacy between Orsino and Viola is not the intimacy of heterosexual lovers – Orsino continues to refer to her as 'Cesario' and she remains in men's clothes – but an unusual closeness between master and servant. Far from registering real knowledge of each other, this suggests that their relationship is based on misrecognition.

OLIVIA, CESARIO AND SEBASTIAN

Olivia's commitment to mourning also seems a kind of self-love, out of which she is shaken by her sudden love for Cesario. Clearly physical looks and youth are a part of her attraction to him, but she falls in love following the urgent power of Cesario's words in the 'willow cabin' speech. Perhaps the extremity of her passion for this youth and her humiliating misinterpretation of 'his' outward appearance is a kind of punishment for her narcissism, mirroring that of Malvolio, but ultimately more benign. She too, however, does not marry the person she thought, unless we are to believe that, in a play so sceptical about outward appearances, Sebastian and Viola are indeed essentially interchangeable.

STUDY FOCUS: SELF-LOVE AND SELFLESS LOVE A02

Malvolio's self-love is commented on by Olivia, and he is soundly punished for his self-regard and for his readiness to believe that 'my lady loves me' (II.5.137). Sir Toby reports that Maria 'adores' him (II.3.151). Sir Andrew's ineffectual suit of Olivia seems to have little passion in it although he does report that he, too, 'was adored once' (II.3.153). Feste's songs in Act II Scene 3 – 'O mistress mine' and 'What is love' – provide a more cynical view of love, and one that is tied inexorably to suffering. He tells of a lover 'slain by a fair cruel maid' (II.4.52) amid the scene between Orsino and Viola in which they discuss the different properties of men's and women's love. Orsino argues that no woman could bear the 'beating of so strong a passion/ As love doth give my heart' (II.4.90–1); Viola counters with a vehement defence of women's silent constancy, displacing her own situation on to her patient sister who 'never told her love' (line 106). It is striking, however, that the one constant, selfless love, that of Antonio for Sebastian, cannot find a place in the general rejoicing at the end of the play. It is not part of the relentless move towards heterosexual marriage, so that Antonio, like Malvolio and Feste, remains outside the celebrations.

A UNION OF SOULS

Ultimately, perhaps the most profound symbol of love as the union of two persons into one is the reunited twins, Viola and Sebastian. So alike that they are like a 'division' of one, 'An apple cleft in twain' (V.1.206–7) – and Shakespeare, as the father of twins himself, must have known that this was very unlikely to be literally true – they represent the union of souls. Platonic theory held that everyone had lost part of themselves and that life was a search for that missing part: Sebastian's and Viola's miraculous restoration represents the reuniting of a single self, rather than the meeting of distinct individuals. The gradual awestruck realisation of what each scarcely dares believe could be true (V.1.210–42) is a more profound coming together than the rather perfunctory proposal of marriage by Orsino to Viola, or the mistaken identities that prompt Olivia's marriage to Sebastian.

KEY QUOTATION: LOVE AND SELF-LOVE A01

Viola: 'Hallow your name to the reverberate hills,/ And make the babbling gossip of the air/ Cry out "Olivia!"' (I.5.227–8)

- Viola describes her answer to Olivia's question, 'Why, what would you?' (I.5.223), as a voice echoing (or reverberating) in the landscape.

- In another reference to echoing in Act II Scene 4, Viola, responding to Feste's melancholy song, tells Orsino, 'It gives a very echo to the seat/ Where love is throned' (lines 19–20).

- At the key moment in this same scene, as Viola asserts female understanding in the face of Orsino's male arrogance, her words then actually chime with and echo his (see II.4.97–101). Here the reference to 'echoing' is then enacted in the text itself through the repetition and rhyme of key words (owe/know/know/owe).

CONTEXT A04

The theme of self-love is linked to parallels in the play to the myth of Echo and Narcissus in Ovid's *Metamorphoses*, in which the nymph, Echo, can only repeat the words of her love, Narcissus, who becomes transfixed by the beauty of his own reflection in a pool and so wastes away. In *Twelfth Night*, unlike Ovid's nymph, however, Viola's 'echo' at these two moments turns the attention of the Duke and Countess towards *her* and so Orsino and Olivia begin to escape their self-involvement.

GENDER

CHECK THE FILM A03

In Trevor Nunn's 1996 film, the intimacy between Orsino and Cesario tips into sexual attraction, and we watch the Duke struggling with his feelings for a young boy. Viola's revelation at the end of the play comes as a great relief to him and, now she is a woman, he can indulge his feelings for her – or him.

VIOLA'S DISGUISE

Viola's disguise, which affects all the characters in Illyria, can be read to suggest that women's roles are over-circumscribed by gender convention and social rules, and that genuine affection cannot flourish in such artificial confines. By being a man with Orsino she is really able to get to know him on more like equal terms and to be sure of her love for him. Certainly Orsino and Cesario become intimate through the freedom offered by her disguise. Whereas Olivia remains for Orsino a remote ideal (he doesn't even do his wooing in person, preferring to send a servant), Cesario/Viola quickly becomes a trusted confidant.

SEXUAL POSSIBILITIES

Much of the humour in performance can derive from the play's repeated flirtation with an apparently homosexual attraction which, in the end, it realigns with the conventions of heterosexual romantic comedy. It is a play fascinated with sexual possibilities, and in this respect it is strikingly modern: a woman falls in love with a character we know to be a woman, and a man falls in love with a character he believes to be a man – and it exploits these situations for comedy before sorting everything out. Perhaps the success of Viola's disguise suggests that gender identity is in the eye of the beholder – a man is someone recognised as and treated as a man, rather than someone with a set biological identity. This is a radical thought: in a society like Elizabethan England, in which the superiority of the male and the inferiority of the female was a cultural given, taking on male clothing and with it male authority could be rather challenging. Perhaps Viola's disguise tests the boundaries of gender, rather than simply following them. As Diana Rigg, who played Viola in 1966, commented later: 'I think the really clever thing that Shakespeare posed … is a sexuality which is not based on the extremes of feminism or masculinism that we have nowadays.'

STUDY FOCUS: CONSERVATIVE OR RADICAL? A02

Many recent critics have discussed whether Shakespeare's use of cross-dressed heroines within the context of all-male acting companies is ultimately conservative or radical in its attitude to gender roles (see **Part Five: Contexts and Critical Debates**). Does

Viola's intimacy with Orsino gained through her disguise suggest that the conventions about courtship are foolish restriction, or does the fact that she uses her disguise as a man to pursue romance – the 'feminine' sphere – rather than something more challenging to masculine authority actually reinforce gender conventions? What do you think? Justify your views with reference to the text.

FEMALE ROLES PLAYED BY BOYS

On the Elizabethan stage, Viola would have been played by a boy actor: there were no women actors on the public stage until the Restoration in 1660 (see **Part Five: Contexts and Critical Debates**, on **Historical Background**). Many of Shakespeare's comedies, including *The Two Gentlemen of Verona*, *As You Like It* and *The Merchant of Venice*, play on this fact. It is thought that these boy actors must have been extremely good and convincing as women, but still, the awareness that underneath this role was a male actor must have been there. Rather than suppressing or ignoring this physical fact, Shakespeare seems to enjoy playing on the confusions it engenders (**pun** intended).

THERE IS NO DARKNESS BUT IGNORANCE

CHECK THE PLAY A03

The 2012 Globe production used an all-male cast and costumes, music and staging which attempted to recreate the 'original practice' of Elizabethan theatre. An interesting effect of the absence of women onstage was that the men playing female roles, including Mark Rylance, used a restrained and stylised artifice in their movement which was at times reminiscent of Japanese Kabuki theatre (a theatrical form in which men play the female roles and which, coincidentally, arose at the very time *Twelfth Night* was written).

KEY QUOTATION: GENDER   A01

Orsino: 'Cesario come –/ For so you shall be while you are a man,/ But when in other habits you are seen,/ Orsino's mistress, and his fancy's queen.' (V.1.362–5)

- In his closing remarks Orsino still addresses Viola as his male page and makes the last of several references in the final scene to her 'masculine usurped attire' (V.1.234), 'maiden weeds' (V.1.239), 'woman's weeds' (V.1.257) and 'maid's garments' (V.1.259).

- Orsino's union with Viola is linked to her appearing in her own clothes, but the Captain who held them is imprisoned at the end by none other than Malvolio, and so the return of her clothes relies on the character who has exited threatening revenge.

- Other of Shakespeare's cross-dressed heroines such as *As You Like It*'s Rosalind or Portia in *The Merchant of Venice* re-establish their femininity at the end of the play by returning in their female clothes, but not so Viola.

- In refusing to re-admit a feminine Viola at its conclusion, the play seems reluctant to relinquish its festivity, the social and sexual topsy-turvy of **carnival** (see **Themes**, on **Twelfth Night**).

CONTEXT A04

Agreement as to the causes of 'madness' have differed widely over the centuries. In ancient times, madness – or its effect in the sense of mental disorder – was often associated with supernatural spirits, but also as a response to bodily illness. Although Freud and others like him are widely-credited with connecting 'madness' to childhood events or trauma, even as far back as Roman times doctors linked the debilitating effects of mental illness to strong or over-powering emotions. It could be argued that it is trauma of one kind or another that leads Olivia (bereavement), Sebastian (loss of his sister) and Malvolio (the victim of a trick) to behave in what might be seen as extraordinary ways.

MADNESS

ILLYRIA – A MAD WORLD

The words 'mad', 'madness' and 'madman' together appear around forty times, more than in any other Shakespeare play, and this frequency registers *Twelfth Night*'s preoccupation

with the topic. As events spiral into bewilderment, characters revert to the only apparent explanation for this irrationality: madness. Feste tells Olivia that Sir Toby's drunkenness makes him 'a madman' (I.5.114). Malvolio asks the revellers, 'My masters, are you mad?' (II.3.75). Olivia recognises that her quick love for Cesario is a kind of 'madness' making her 'as mad as he [Malvolio]' (III.4.14). Sebastian wonders if he is 'mad' when Olivia addresses him so fondly (IV.1.54 and again at IV.3.15), and muses on whether it is in fact she who is mad (IV.3.16). Malvolio pleads with 'Sir Topas', 'do not think I am mad' (IV.2.25), and Feste continues to taunt him 'are you not mad indeed/ or do you but counterfeit?' (IV.2.96–7); his letter to Olivia is signed 'The madly used Malvolio' (V.1.290). Feste's habitual title for Olivia, 'madonna', seems designed to echo the word mad, as at I.5.93 and I.5.113.

STUDY FOCUS: IN THE DARK A02

Madness is an aspect of the topsy-turvydom that governs the play (see **Themes**, on **Twelfth Night**), and is related to the comedy of mistaken identities around the separated twins. In Malvolio's case, however, this **metaphorical** madness, used to suggest a kind of incomprehension or irrationality, comes close to psychological breakdown, as he is pushed almost beyond sanity by the merciless Feste. As with many aspects of the play, the theme has its light, comic side but also a darker reverse.

REVISION FOCUS: TASK 4 A02

How far do you agree with the following statements?

● Whilst 'mad' behaviour governs the play, by the end order and sanity are restored.

● Madness is predominantly associated with love in the play.

Try writing opening paragraphs for essays based on these discussion points. Set out your arguments clearly.

STRUCTURE

DRAMATIC STRUCTURE

TWO PLOTS

One key to the success of *Twelfth Night* is its skilful construction. The play's structure is built from a main plot involving the twins Viola and Sebastian (linked to Orsino and Olivia) and also a sub-plot involving the 'gulling' of Malvolio (linked to Sir Toby and his companions), which is itself underpinned by the 'gulling' of Sir Andrew by Sir Toby, a practice which has already begun before the play starts.

The two plots and their different elements intersect in Act III Scene 4 with the trickery against Malvolio and the mock duel between Sir Andrew and Viola. Following the careful construction of the different intrigues and plots, Shakespeare creates a triumphant centrepiece to the play; the increasingly manic action gathers pace to end in mayhem which is brought to an abrupt halt by the arrival of Antonio quickly followed by the Officers. The solution to the madness appears in the following scene, which begins with Feste addressing Sebastian as Cesario. A key to the success of this climactic scene, therefore, lies not only in the dialogue and business it contains, but in the play's construction.

STUDY FOCUS: JUXTAPOSITION   A02

The two plots of the play allow Shakespeare to make extensive use of the structural technique of **juxaposition**, in which one scene is followed by another which is in stark contrast to it. For example, Act IV Scene 2 with Malvolio isolated in the dark dungeon is immediately followed by a scene with a **soliloquy** from Sebastian which begins with 'This is the air, that is the glorous sun' (IV.3.1). The two plots allow more fundamental parallels and contrasts to be drawn between characters and situations. For example, Act II Scene 4 which ends with Orsino despatching Viola to continue his self-indulgent wooing of Olivia is followed by one which starts with Malvolio vainly fantasising about marrying the Countess. Each character, with the exception of Feste, is linked to the main or sub-plot, creating a variety of narrative threads which enrich and extend the play's dramatic and comic possibilities. Examine the play for other examples where Shakespeare juxtaposes scenes to create parallels and contrasts and to change the mood.

CONSTRUCTING THE COMEDY

In *Twelfth Night*, Shakespeare places scenes carefully in sequence, often to create **dramatic irony** in which the audience knows more than the characters and also to maintain the comic tone. So, for example, the scene in which Viola realises that Olivia has fallen in love with her is immediately preceded by the appearance of Sebastian, allowing the audience to enjoy her predicament in the knowledge that there is a solution to it. Shakespeare also prepares key moments in the action, by having characters mentioned or discussed by others before they appear, delaying the entrance to build up the audience's anticipation, for example in the case of the first appearance of Olivia, or of Malvolio in yellow stockings and-cross garters.

MUSIC

Music begins and ends the play. It also punctuates the action as a commentary on characters and situations and to change the mood. In this sense it is an important aspect of the play's structure. Shakespeare even juxtaposes different types of music, the raucous late-night revelling of Sir Toby, Sir Andrew and Feste of Act II Scene 3 being followed in the next scene by Feste's haunting 'Come away, death' sung to Orsino and Cesario.

CHECK THE BOOK   A03

Kiernan Ryan, in *Shakespeare's Comedies* (2009), provides a superb summary of some of the main links between *Twelfth Night* and Shakespeare's previous comedies, such as *The Comedy of Errors* (see pp. 236–40). He also shows how Shakespeare's plundering of his previous work for *Twelfth Night* does not involve the comedies alone, demonstrating, for instance, how Malvolio recalls similar 'scapegoat figures' such as Shylock in *The Merchant of Venice*, or how his antithesis Sir Toby reminds us of Falstaff (in *Henry IV* and *The Merry Wives of Windsor*).

CHECK THE FILM   A03

Directors sometimes change the order of the scenes as set out in the First Folio, with mixed results. In his 1996 film, Trevor Nunn makes the scene in which Malvolio gives the ring to Cesario follow on from the previous scene between Olivia and Viola, postponing the appearance of the scene with Sebastian. This decision creates realistic continuity which is helpful in film, but also removes layers of dramatic irony.

GRADE BOOSTER A02

The form of a literary work means its shape and structure and its style and conventions. Form also means the type of work the piece is – for example, short story, poem or essay. In this case the form is a play in the genre and conventions of romantic comedy.

FORM

THE COMEDY GENRE

SHAKESPEARE'S COMEDIES

Twelfth Night is listed under Comedies in the First Folio of 1623, although this is a category which also included the 'late' plays such as *The Tempest* and *The Winter's Tale* and what have been called the 'problem' plays (since they defy ready generic categorising) such as *All's Well That Ends Well* and *Measure for Measure*. *Twelfth Night* is usually regarded as the last example of Shakespeare's use of a form of romantic comedy which also includes *As You Like It* and *Love's Labour's Lost*. A distinctive feature of *Twelfth Night*, however, is how in this comedy he combines humour with **pathos**, laughter with melancholy.

It was the law student John Manningham who noted very early (in 1602) the way *Twelfth Night* borrowed from *The Comedy of Errors* and, in the world of Illyria, Shakespeare takes the **tropes** and **motifs** from his previous comedies, such as identical twins, the girl disguised as a boy and mock duels, and extends their boundaries, for example making the 'identical' twins male and female.

LOVE'S PERMUTATIONS

Another distinctive aspect of *Twelfth Night* is how Shakespeare, through Viola's disguise, extends the boundaries of romantic comedy itself to play with different gender permutations, boy-girl, boy-boy, girl-girl. The tension and inverted erotic interplay between the different characters is kept up throughout since Shakespeare postpones the conventional resolution of romantic comedy through marriage until some time after the end of the drama. As Jan Kott says in *Shakespeare Our Contemporary* (1974), 'In Illyria ambiguity is the principle of love as well as of comedy.'

MALVOLIO: A TRAGIC HERO?

For John Manningham the most memorable feature of the comedy is the practice against Malvolio and even King Charles I, in his copy of the Second Folio, amended the text by writing Malvolio in place of Shakespeare's own title. The figure of Olivia's grave but vain steward looms large over the comedy, as a threat to the mirth and revelry. Some critics have seen him, through his exposure and humiliation, as a tragic character. His name, however, indicates his place in the comic scheme and his come-uppance, though cruel and pathetic, is not tragic since he lacks the wisdom which tragic characters achieve before their end, failing to grow in insight and humanity. Instead of being a tragic hero, he threatens to become the anti-hero in a tragedy, as he exits promising revenge. At this point in the play, Malvolio not only leaves, he breaks the boundaries of the comic genre to create a moment of unresolved discord.

CRITICAL VIEWPOINT A03

In *Elia's Essays* (1823), Charles Lamb questioned the function of Olivia's steward as a comic character saying, 'Malvolio is not essentially ludicrous … He becomes comic by accident … his pride, or his gravity (call it which you will) is inherent and native to the man, not mock or affected, which latter only are the fit objects to excite laughter'.

STUDY FOCUS: LOOSE ENDS?   A01

Although Shakespeare promised *What You Will*, the end of *Twelfth Night* is not the conventionally happy and comfortable resolution that we might expect from romantic comedy. In the romantic pairings there are astonishing revelations; Malvolio has exited; Antonio is overlooked; Sir Andrew is wounded, disillusioned and out of pocket; Sir Toby is punished; even Viola's Captain remains imprisoned. The focus of the comic denouement is rather the miraculous restoration of the twins, which is precisely not comic, but tender and moving.

LANGUAGE

VERSE AND STYLE

BLANK VERSE AND PROSE

Twelfth Night is written in a mixture of **blank verse** and prose, and it is always worth looking at the shifts between these two modes. It has been argued that Elizabethans were as subconsciously sensitive to **pentameter** cadences as we are to certain jazz or other musical **rhythms**, and thus that alterations in this verbal tempo would be more readily registered by Shakespeare's own audience than by modern readers. Prose is often given to speakers of lower rank or for passages of comic or bawdy exchange: it is characteristic of this division that Sir Toby Belch and Sir Andrew Aguecheek usually speak in prose, and that Malvolio follows this at his entry into their revels of Act II Scene 3, whereas Malvolio speaks verse to Olivia when he pulls himself up to his full height to reassert his wounded dignity in the final act. Olivia and Viola both speak prose during Act I Scene 5, but break into verse speech in the same scene and elsewhere.

IMAGERY

In a good play the dramatist seeks to make the ideas, characters and developments vivid and memorable. One way of achieving this is to link, for example, a character or situation with certain qualities or activities. When these **images** occur in the play, they trigger associations and connotations which help the audience to remember and come to a fuller understanding of the character or predicament. In Shakespeare's more mature works, particularly, imagery provides texture, richness and density, setting off chain reactions of ideas and associations which are inexhaustible and infinitely varied since the associations arising are also affected by the varied experiences of each member of the audience.

Individual images are striking, such as Viola's 'sister', really herself, as being 'like Patience on a monument,/ Smiling at grief' (II.4.110–11). The images also function in strands and webs which help to connect, reinforce and enliven the shifts in the play as a whole. So, for instance, this image of 'Patience' is preceded by an image of sickness which is part of a network of such imagery in the play, which even includes Sir Andrew's name, Aguecheek: 'She never told her love,/ But let concealment like a worm i' th'bud/ Feed on her damask cheek' (II.4.106–8). The flower is being quietly killed in its 'youth' before it has had time to bloom. The imagery here conveys the power of Viola's love and suggests that it is secretly consuming her.

STUDY FOCUS: COMPLEX IMAGES   A01

Some other interweaving strands which could be explored include imagery of music, time, youth and age, art and nature, flowers, food and drink, appetite and eating, clothes and disguise, acting and the theatre, the weather, confinement and prison, money, souls and spirits, jewels, the sea and salt water (tears) and, of course, language and speech (gossip). It is not surprising in a Shakespearean romantic comedy that the play is also full of bawdy imagery. Now follow some of these threads. Shakespeare always repays such investigations and you will deepen your understanding of the play and make new and exciting discoveries that no one has found before.

CHECK THE BOOK   A03

The first systematic attempt to analyse Shakespeare's language was Caroline Spurgeon's *Shakespeare's Imagery and What It Tells Us*, first published in 1935 and frequently reprinted. Spurgeon notes that the balanced language of *Twelfth Night* reflects and projects the bitter-sweet tone of the whole play. Some of the most memorable images come from the play's love poetry, such as the famous opening lines, but these are balanced out by robust **similes** such as Sir Andrew's limp hair hanging 'like flax on a distaff' (I.3.84).

SEEMING AND BEING

In *Shakespeare's Language* (2000), Frank Kermode discusses the importance to *Twelfth Night* of the idea of impersonation and the attempt to discriminate between what actually *is* and what *seems*. This clearly operates as a plot device, but Kermode also argues that it works on a linguistic level too. Viola's reminder to herself that she is 'not that I play' (I.5.153) infects other self-identifications, so that doubt and circumlocution seem to surround the play's characters. Olivia replies to her question, 'Are you the lady of the house?' in unnecessarily evasive terms, 'If I do not usurp myself, I am' (I.5.153–4). Malvolio's trick letter bears the postscript 'Thou canst not choose but know who I am' (II.5.143–4); Sir Andrew's challenge addresses his assailant Cesario as 'Youth, whatsoever thou art, thou art but a scurvy fellow' (III.4.125–6). By means of these evasive namings and self-namings, the play's language develops the plot of mistaken identity, but it also approaches a philosophical interest in the relation between things and their names and the difficulty of language ever being truly accurate.

STUDY FOCUS: FESTE AND LANGUAGE   AO2

It is Feste who provides a philosophical perspective on the relation between language and thought and language and things. In his conversation with Viola he continually quibbles on the meaning of words and then uses the **image** of the 'cheveril glove' (III.1.9–10) to suggest how malleable and therefore untrustworthy language can be. He says that language has become debased and calls words 'rascals' (III.1.17). When Viola asks for his reason he answers, 'Truth, sir, I can yield you none without words, and words are grown so false, I am loath to prove reason with them' (III.1.20–1). In *William Shakespeare* (1986), Terry Eagleton neatly summarises this conundrum: 'Reason, the form of reality, can be articulated only in words and yet is disfigured by them. Without language there can be no reason, but no reason with it either' (see p. 28). Similarly when Feste, imitating the parson, torments the imprisoned Malvolio, '"That that is, is", so I, being Master Parson, am Master Parson; for what is "that" but "that" and "is" but "is"?' (IV.2.13–14), it is words which make Malvolio's prison and threaten to overwhelm his sense of who he is. Feste's self-confessed role as 'corrupter of words' (III.1.30) is, throughout, the source of his power.

HISTORICAL BACKGROUND

SHAKESPEARE'S AGE

THE RENAISSANCE

Shakespeare arrived in London at the very time that the Elizabethan period was poised to become the 'golden age' of English literature. Although Elizabeth reigned as queen from 1558 to 1603, the term 'Elizabethan' is used very loosely in a literary sense to refer to the period 1580–1625 when the great works of the age were produced. (Sometimes the later part of this period is distinguished as 'Jacobean', from the Latin form of the name of Elizabeth's successor, James VI of Scotland and I of England, who reigned from 1603 to 1625.)

The poet Edmund Spenser heralded the new literary age with his pastoral poem *The Shepheardes Calender* (1579), and in his essay *An Apologie for Poetrie* (written in about 1580 and published in 1595), his patron Sir Philip Sidney championed the imaginative power of the 'speaking picture of poetry', famously declaring that 'Nature never set forth the earth in so rich a tapestry as divers poets have done … Her world is brazen, the poets only deliver a golden.' Spenser and Sidney were part of that rejuvenating movement in European culture which since the nineteenth century has been known as the Renaissance. Meaning literally 'rebirth' it denotes a revival and redirection of artistic and intellectual endeavour which began in Italy in the fourteenth century and reached England in the early sixteenth century. Its keynote was a curiosity in thought which challenged the old assumptions and traditions: as the poet John Donne was to put it in 'An Anatomy of the World' (1633), 'new Philosophy calls all in doubt'. To the innovative spirit of the Renaissance, the preceding ages appeared dully unoriginal and conformist, what the critic C. S. Lewis has termed 'the drab age'.

CHANGES THAT INFLUENCED SHAKESPEARE

The Renaissance spirit was fuelled by the rediscovery of many classical texts and the culture of Ancient Greece and Rome. This reawakening fostered a confidence in human reason and in human potential which, in every sphere, challenged old convictions. The discovery of America and its peoples (Columbus had sailed in 1492) demonstrated that the world was a larger and stranger place than had been thought. The cosmological speculation of Copernicus (later confirmed by Galileo) that the sun, not the earth, was the centre of the planetary system challenged the centuries-old belief that the earth and human beings were at the centre of the universe. The pragmatic political philosophy of Machiavelli seemed to cut politics free from its traditional link with morality, by advising statesmen to use any means to secure a desired end. The religious movements we know collectively as the Reformation broke with the Roman Catholic church and set the individual conscience, not ecclesiastical authority, at the centre of religious life. Nothing, it seemed, was beyond questioning, nothing impossible, although the fate of the hero of Marlowe's play *Doctor Faustus* showed the limits and dangers of such radical freedom.

CONTEXT **A04**

In the context of *Twelfth Night* and the puritanical Malvolio, and also the eventual closure of the theatres by the Puritans in 1642, it is worth noting that Sidney's *An Apologie for Poetrie* was written in response to a pamphlet entitled *The Schoole of Abuse* written by a former actor turned Puritan called Stephen Gosson, in which Gosson attacked the English stage on ethical grounds as a den of vice. Sidney shifts the terms of the debate on to aesthetic grounds, but actually complains about what becomes a feature of Shakespearean drama, namely the lack of observance of the three dramatic unities (of time, place and action) and the mixing of tragic and comic elements.

CONTEXT **A04**

Machiavelli wrote *The Prince* in 1532. It was a political book that appeared to approve a certain type of political behaviour. His critics claim that he advised political leaders on how to tyrannise their subjects. He also appeared to accept immoral and criminal acts and disregard the needs of individuals.

CONTEXT **A04**

In the late sixteenth century, a number of young men who had been to the universities of Oxford and Cambridge came to London in the 1580s and began to write plays based on their knowledge of classical dramas of Ancient Greece and Rome. John Lyly, Christopher Marlowe and Thomas Kyd wrote full-length plays on secular (non-religious) subjects, offering a range of **characterisation** and situation hitherto unattempted in English drama. Lyly wrote in prose, but the other playwrights composed in the unrhymed **iambic pentameters** (blank verse) which the Earl of Surrey had introduced into English earlier in the sixteenth century. This was a freer and more expressive medium than the rhymed verse of medieval drama.

'RENAISSANCE' OR 'EARLY MODERN'?

The term 'Renaissance' suggests that this age defined itself in relation to the past. Some historians and literary scholars have preferred to use a term which stresses the period's relationship to the future: 'early modern'. Whereas the idea of the Renaissance focuses on intellectual and artistic developments, the early modern period stresses those features of life more familiar to us now – with changing ideas of society, of family, of sexuality and the roles of men and women, with the operations of class or rank, with urban life, economics and questions of personal and cultural identity.

NEGATIVE CAPABILITY

Another major influence on European thought was Michel de Montaigne whose essays were first published in French in 1580 and then with additional material in 1588. They were translated into English by John Florio, a lexicographer, writer and language teacher, and published in 1603. Montaigne's ability to consider different viewpoints together with his balanced humanism produced ideas and positions which are continually surprising and non-judgemental. These characteristics are evident not only in specific speeches in Shakespeare's plays, but also in the overriding nature of his genius as a playwright, which the poet John Keats called his 'Negative Capability … that is when man is capable of being in uncertainties. Mysteries, doubts, without any irritable reaching after fact and reason.' In this context, *Twelfth Night* itself has a strange quality of suspension,

Illyria being a world where, for a time, normal rules, assumptions and relationships are up in the air and where resolution is postponed until some time after the play has ended.

STUDY FOCUS: SHAKESPEARE THE INNOVATOR **A04**

Shakespeare's drama is a product of its age, as well as of its creator, and is innovative and challenging. It interrogates (examines and asks questions of) the beliefs, assumptions and politics upon which Elizabethan society was founded. And although the plays often conclude in a restoration of order and stability, many critics are inclined to argue that their imaginative energy goes into subverting, rather than reinforcing, traditional values such as, for example, ideas about gender in *Twelfth Night*.

SHAKESPEARE'S THEATRE

The theatre for which Shakespeare wrote his plays was a distinctly Elizabethan invention. There had been no theatres or acting companies during the medieval period, when plays – usually on religious subjects – were performed by travelling groups of players in market-places, inn yards and in the halls of great houses. Such actors were regarded by the authorities as little better than vagabonds and layabouts.

A PROFESSIONAL THEATRE

Another influence on the establishment of a professional theatre was a new law forbidding travelling players unless they were under the patronage of a nobleman. (Shakespeare's company was under the patronage of the Lord Chamberlain.) This system ensured that only the best troupes survived, and that their activity centred on London, where their patrons attended the queen at her court. In 1576 the entrepreneur James Burbage built the first permanent playhouse, called 'The Theatre', in Shoreditch just beyond London's northern boundary. Other theatre buildings followed, mostly just outside the city walls or on the south bank of the river Thames to avoid the regulations of London's civic authorities. The design of these playhouses was based on that of bear-baiting arenas, and the theatre continued to be associated with this popular bloodsport. The theatre was not the respectable middle-class institution of modern times: it was identified with prostitution, pickpocketing and with the spread of plague. It was blamed for encouraging idleness and criminality, and some extreme preachers argued that the whole system of acting was a form of lying and therefore of sin. Local residents complained about the numbers of people who congregated at the theatre, and, when carriages became popular in the Jacobean period, the congestion on London Bridge caused by playgoers prompted the first parking regulations.

Shakespeare's company performed at Burbage's Theatre until 1596, and also used the Swan and Curtain theatres until moving into their own new building, the Globe, in 1599. It was burned down in 1613 when the thatched roof was ignited by a spark from a cannon fired during a performance of Shakespeare's *Henry VIII*. The Globe Theatre has recently been reconstructed, using the available evidence, on Bankside, which offers some sense of the experience of theatregoing for Shakespeare's audiences.

FORM AND STRUCTURE

The arrival of Shakespeare as a playwright came after the appearance of public theatres in London. The form of the Elizabethan theatre is thought to be derived from the inn yards and animal-baiting rings which provided other kinds of entertainment. They were circular wooden buildings with a paved courtyard in the middle open to the sky. A rectangular stage jutted out into the yard, or pit, where some audience members paid a penny to stand and watch the play. Round the perimeter of the yard were tiered galleries, covered with thatch, providing more expensive seats for wealthier spectators. Performances took place in the afternoons to make use of daylight. The yard was just over 24 metres in diameter, the stage measured 12 by 9 metres at 1.67 metres high, and the theatre could hold about 3,000 spectators. The stage itself was partially covered by a roof or canopy which projected from the wall at the rear of the stage and was supported by two posts at the front. Two doors at the back of the stage led into the dressing room (or 'tiring house') and it was by means of these doors that actors entered and left the stage. Between the doors was a small recess or alcove which was curtained off to provide a 'discovery space', and over the discovery space was a balcony. In the early years of the seventeenth century, Shakespeare's company acquired a smaller indoor theatre called Blackfriars which could seat about 700 people. As a more expensive venue, this theatre probably catered to an audience of a higher social rank. Blackfriars had facilities for more elaborate stage and lighting effects, including a machine for lowering actors from above the stage, and these new possibilities were incorporated in Shakespeare's late plays.

CRITICAL VIEWPOINT A03

There are different theories about how the form of Elizabethan theatres developed: the influence of medieval amphitheatres for animal sports is only one suggestion. Frances A. Yates, in her book *Theatre of the World* (1969), argues powerfully for the influence of a Rennaissance return to the ancient theatre and classical models. The very name chosen for James Burbage's first permanent playhouse, 'The Theatre', suggests such a link.

CRITICAL VIEWPOINT A03

Bertolt Brecht, who was heavily influenced by Shakespeare, developed a theory called 'distanciation' (*Verfremdungseffekt*, sometimes translated as 'alienation') in which the audience is made aware that they are watching a play, and the familiar and obvious are made strange again to reawaken the audience's enquiry and curiosity about the characters and situations depicted. The style of acting in a Brecht play does not involve 'becoming' the character, but 'performing' it. In this context, Viola's disguise in *Twelfth Night* could be regarded as a 'distancing' effect, in which the audience is constantly reminded that she is playing a role. Can you find any other examples of 'distanciation' in *Twelfth Night*?

STAGING PRACTICES

There was little in the way of large-scale scenery, which is why Shakespeare's characters often tell us in detail where they are or what their surroundings are like or that it is dark or dawn or stormy. As locations were not represented visually, they have more power as **symbolic** places, perhaps suggesting an inner landscape or psychological state rather than a specific geographical place. Props and costumes were probably also limited. All the roles, including those of women, were played by male actors. This is particularly significant for *Twelfth Night*: when Viola dresses in male clothes to become Cesario, the layers of pretence are multiplied as, of course, 'Viola' is played by a male actor in the first place. These factors, together with the form of the playhouse, meant that audiences were always aware that they were watching a play. The drama of the period often draws explicit attention to

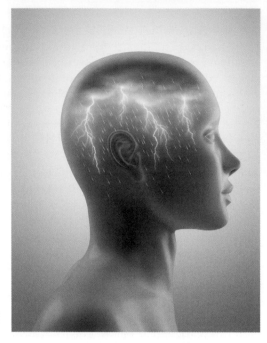

itself *as* drama, using non-naturalistic conventions such as **soliloquy**, the **imagery** of theatrical performance, exploring issues of disguise, role-playing, and the gap between appearance and reality.

STUDY FOCUS: A MICROCOSM   A02

The early modern theatre was not concerned to make its audience believe that what it was watching was really happening – recognising the artificiality of the spectacle was key to the theatrical experience. Modern theatres, by contrast, tend to use lighting and conventions of audience behaviour to encourage spectators to forget themselves as they

become absorbed by the action on stage. The auditorium is usually dark, with a passive, silent and attentive audience watching a spotlit stage where actors are vocal, demonstrative and dramatic. By all accounts, Shakespeare's theatre was quite different. Audience members went to be seen as much as to see, they were lit by natural light like the actors and wore the same kind of clothing. They had none of our modern deference, arriving late, talking and heckling during the performance, eating, drinking and conducting business. It was all much more like our experience of pantomime, where the artificiality of its conventions is enjoyed, expected and understood. But calling a theatre 'the Globe' suggests that it is a microcosm of the world, and the theatre did provide Elizabethan culture with a **metaphor** for understanding its own existence, as in Shakespeare's own famous observation, 'All the world's a stage' (*As You Like It*).

LITERARY BACKGROUND

SHAKESPEARE'S SOURCES

Shakespeare hardly ever invented his own plots – attitudes to literary originality were then rather different from our own views – preferring to take episodes and narratives from existing stories, often translations from European languages. His method in writing *Twelfth Night* was no different. The ultimate source for the play is an Italian drama called *Gl'Ingannati* (The Deceived Ones), performed in Siena in 1531 and reprinted numerous times during the century. We do not know, however, whether Shakespeare had access to this text in its original form. It is more likely that he knew of it at second, or even third hand, via Barnabe Riche's prose tale of Apolonius and Silla, part of his *Farewell to the Military Profession* (1581). Riche's story, in outline, is of Apolonius, a young duke visiting Cyprus where the daughter of his host, Silla, falls in love with him but cannot get him to notice her. Apolonius leaves Cyprus for his home. Silla follows him by boat but is the only survivor of a shipwreck. She disguises herself as a man, assumes the name of her brother, Silvio, currently serving as a soldier in Africa, and gets herself a position at Apolonius's court. Apolonius is courting a wealthy widow, Julina, and sends Silla as his messenger. Julina falls in love with Silla. When the real Silvio arrives to search for his sister, Julina mistakes him for the Duke's messenger and spends the night with him, conceiving a child as a result. Silvio leaves the city, and Julina claims Silla as the father. Silla is so amazed at this claim that she confesses her real identity to Julina, who tells Apolonius, who is so impressed by Silla's devotion to him that he marries her. The real Silvio hears of the situation and, stricken with remorse about Julina, marries her. All live happily ever after.

> **CONTEXT** **A04**
>
> The sub-plot involving Malvolio is Shakespeare's addition to the original story of the tale of Apolonius and Silla in Barnabe Riche's *Farewell to the Military Profession*. The conflict between Malvolio and the revellers in Act II Scene 3 is seen similar to an actual event which came before the court of the Star Chamber in the winter of 1601, involving one Sir Thomas Posthumus Huby, the husband of Lady Sidney, and a group of drunken Yorkshire squires who came to party at his wife's house.

SHAKESPEARE'S ADAPTATION

Shakespeare's main adaptation of the story is to simplify it – Viola does not already know Orsino, as Silla does Apolonius. He also romanticises it – Olivia falls quickly in love with Sebastian and their marriage is indeed hasty, but it precedes a sexual encounter between them. Shakespeare also makes use of his own play *The Comedy of Errors*, as John Manningham noted (see **Part One: Introducing *Twelfth Night***, on ***Twelfth Night* in Context**). In this play, confusion over the identities of twins predominates, including Antonio's mistaken request for money from the wrong twin, Viola, in Act III Scene 4.

REVISION FOCUS: TASK 5 **A03**

How far do you agree with the following statements?

- Shakespeare's comedies make powerful use of the plot device of twins for dramatic effect.
- The shipwrecks that open both *The Tempest* and *Twelfth Night* launch emotional after-effects that last throughout each play.

Try writing opening paragraphs for essays based on these discussion points. Set out your arguments clearly.

COMPARING *TWELFTH NIGHT* WITH OTHER TEXTS

Some of the links between *Twelfth Night* and Shakespeare's other comedies, including *As You Like It* and *The Comedy of Errors*, are discussed in these Notes. The love triangle between Olivia, Orsino and Viola can also be closely related to the situation between the man, the youth and the woman in Shakespeare's *Sonnets*. Rich and imaginative comparisons between *Twelfth Night* and a vast array of texts by other writers can be drawn in terms of ideas, genre, character, language and theme and a very few suggestions are given below.

PLAYS

Parallels between Oscar Wilde's romantic comedy *The Importance of Being Earnest* (1895) and *Twelfth Night* can be drawn in terms of genre, characters and also through themes such as language, identity, narcissism and desire. For example, in *Twelfth Night* the clash between revelry (Sir Toby and his companions) and restraint (Malvolio) could be linked in Wilde's comedy to the clash between the need for moral respectability, reinforced through religion (Dr Chasuble), education (Miss Prism) and society (Lady Bracknell), and the desire for pleasure and freedom. Viola's choice of a male disguise as Cesario, which underlies the mayhem in *Twelfth Night*, could be compared and contrasted with the adoption of different names and identities by Jack and Algernon, who become Ernest and Bunbury to escape their social confines and moral obligations. Comic confusions and mistakes abound before Jack's true identity is revealed (Ernest) and the romantic pairings can take place.

POETRY

The key to making links between love poetry and *Twelfth Night* will be to go beyond the generic to draw precise and detailed comparisons and parallels. Much love poetry considers the endurance of love and desire in the face of mortality, the passing of time and the transience of physical beauty, from Andrew Marvell's *To His Coy Mistress* (compare this for instance to the similar message, but very different tone of Feste's *O, Mistress Mine*) to Philip Larkin's 'An Arundel Tomb' (1964) or Gillian Clarke's 'My Box'. The idea of a union of souls in love is expressed in the poetry of John Donne, such as *A Valediction Forbidding Mourning*, or Sir Philip Sidney's *My True Love Hath My Heart* to Shelley's *Love's Philosophy*. Robert Browning's poetry explores themes of love, desire and madness. In *Two in the Campagna* the speaker expresses an endless yearning to become completely at one with his lover and achieve total communion. These poems could be linked with the idea in *Twelfth Night* of love as a 'solemn combination of … souls' (V.1.360–1) and the restoration of Sebastian and Viola as 'One face, one voice, one habit, and two persons' (V.1.200). Music and song are a means by which Shakespeare changes the mood and tone of the drama, their importance to love being signalled from the very start of the play, and the reader will wish to select personal examples of love songs and poems which link with the play.

NOVELS

Novels which might be linked with *Twelfth Night* include Jane Austen's *Emma* (1816), *Pride and Prejudice* (1813) or *Sense and Sensibility* (1811). Taking *Emma* as an example, the eponymous heroine's precocity could be compared with the lack of self-knowledge of Olivia and Orsino. Her presumptuous efforts at match-making lead to complications and intrigues in the lives and loves of the people around her, before she comes to develop a deeper understanding of herself and others and discovers love. You could consider Viola in relation to other female characters who remain silent about their love, such as Jane Eyre in the novel by Charlotte Brontë. Illuminating comparisons can be made in terms of gender identity and cross-dressing between *Twelfth Night* and, for example, Virginia Woolf's *Orlando* (1928) or between love, obsession and madness in Ian McEwan's *Enduring Love* (1997). *The French Lieutenant's Woman* by John Fowles (1969) can be linked with *Twelfth Night* not only through themes of love and identity, but also in the way each work calls attention to itself as fiction and artefact, questioning the relationship between language and 'reality'.

CHECK THE PLAY A03

A comedy which involves mayhem arising from women disguised as men and 'doubles' is Carlo Goldoni's *A Servant of Two Masters* (1743, see Lee Hall's 2003 translation) or *One Man Two Guvnors* by Richard Bean (2011), in which the period Italian setting shifts to Brighton in the 1960s. You could also compare Viola to other cross-dressed heroines in drama, such as Margery Pinchwife in Wycherley's *The Country Wife* (1675), or Hellena in Aphra Behn's *The Rover* (1677–81).

CHECK THE BOOK A03

Carol Ann Duffy explores the love poem in her collections *Rapture* (2005) and *Love Poems* (2010), both of which could be closely linked to *Twelfth Night*, with, for example, 'Anne Hathaway', in which Shakespeare's wife considers his 'will', or lesbian love in 'Warming Her Pearls' and 'Girlfriends', or 'White Writing', an epithalamium (wedding poem) for a marriage between women.

CRITICAL DEBATES

EARLY CRITICS

Early critics of *Twelfth Night*, following John Manningham, took particular note of the Malvolio plot and a play entitled 'Malvolio' was performed in the seventeenth century. Samuel Johnson considered the steward 'truly comic', but criticised the play for its lack of 'credibility' in the matter of Olivia's marriage to Sebastian. For William Hazlitt, the play represented the 'ludicrous', making 'us laugh at the follies of mankind, not despise them, and still less bear any ill-will towards them', and he confessed to a sneaking 'regard for Malvolio'. Johnson's and Hazlitt's critiques are included in D. J. Palmer's *Casebook* on the play (1972). Other early nineteenth-century views are reprinted in Jonathan Bate's collection *The Romantics on Shakespeare* (1992), including the German critic August Schlegel's observation that the play 'unites the entertainment of an intrigue, contrived with great ingenuity, to a rich fund of comic characters and situations and the beauteous colours of ethereal poetry'. Charles Lamb, like Hazlitt, values Malvolio, arguing that 'even in his abused state of chains and darkness, a sort of greatness seems never to desert him', and concluding that the 'catastrophe of this character [has] a kind of tragic interest'.

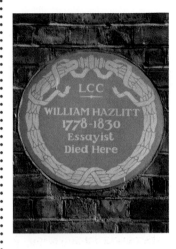

APPROACHES TO THE PLAY

A CROWD-PLEASER

Three basic movements in the history of the literary reception of comedies can be traced. Up until the middle of the twentieth century, comedies were seen as escapist crowd-pleasers, whose unreality was part of their sentimental charm. This critical movement has its clearest expression in the title of John Dover Wilson's, *Shakespeare's Happy Comedies* (1962). Leslie Hotson's influential but ultimately unproven speculation that the play was written for performance at court on 6 January 1600 is also characteristic of this approach. Hotson's opening to his *The First Night of Twelfth Night* (1954) asks merrily, 'Is there anywhere a more delightful comedy than *Twelfth Night*? The cheerful gale of popular favour has sent it down the centuries full-sailed, on a sea of music and laughter.'

SOCIAL MYTHS AND RITUALS

Around the 1950s, critics schooled in anthropological approaches to literature began to examine the comedies in the context of social myths and rituals, which was seen as being particularly important to *Twelfth Night*. C. L. Barber's influential *Shakespeare's Festive Comedy* (1959) relates Elizabethan drama to social customs and holiday comedy, and the chapter on the play identifies its power 'to move audiences through release to clarification, making distinctions between false care and true freedom'.

CHALLENGE TO SOCIAL ORDER

The third aspect of criticism is exemplified in R. S. White's *New Casebook* volume (1996). Here, Geoffrey Hartman argues that the play is so preoccupied by **puns** and witty **rhetoric** that it is language in its slipperiness and vitality that becomes its central theme. In contrast to C. L. Barber, Michael Bristol suggests that the relationship between **carnival** and theatre permanently challenges, rather than endorses, social order. Whereas the essays in the earlier volume stress unity of theme and construction, these later pieces pick out discordant or dissonant elements to stress the play's darker and more problematic aspects.

GENDER AND SEXUALITY

CHECK THE BOOK A03

The play's different and complex depictions of gender and sexuality are discussed in essays by Stephen Greenblatt and Dympna Callaghan. Callaghan challenges the heterosexual assumptions of critics who stress the play's ultimate marriage resolutions while suppressing the troubling desire of Orsino for his page, Olivia for a woman, and Antonio for his young master, and reminds us of the significance of the fact that these plays were originally performed by all-male casts. See R. S. White (ed.), *Twelfth Night: Contemporary Critical Essays* (1996).

The play's representation of gender and sexuality has been one of the most fruitful areas for recent scholarship. In a chapter in his book *Impersonations: The Performance of Gender in Shakespeare's England* (1996), Stephen Orgel stresses the complications of the fact that Viola's part would have originally been played by a male actor. He also examines why Viola opts to disguise herself as a 'eunuch', or castrated male, rather than as a young or immature man.

The play's homoerotic potential is discussed by Valerie Traub in her *Desire and Anxiety: Circulations of Sexuality in Shakespearean Drama* (1992), and by Joseph Pequigney in 'The Two Antonios and Same Sex Love in *The Merchant of Venice* and *Twelfth Night*'. Pequigney discusses the Antonio characters in the two plays: both are identified in passionate, self-sacrificial relation to other men and both are left unmarried and unresolved at the end of their respective play. The essay is reprinted in the collection of Deborah Barker and Ivo Kamps, *Shakespeare and Gender: A History* (1995).

In his book *William Shakespeare* (1986), Terry Eagleton considers questions of language and desire in *Twelfth Night* in the light of Marxism and semiotics (the study of signs and **symbols**). In her book *Still Harping on Daughters: Women and Drama in the Age of Shakespeare* (1989), Lisa Jardine argues that boys playing women's roles is intended to titillate a male audience, and she quotes extensively from contemporary anti-theatrical pamphlets to support this proposition.

THEATRE PRACTITIONERS

Twelfth Night has been a popular play in the theatre, and information from theatre practitioners about the play is an extremely useful aspect of its critical history. Zoë Wanamaker discusses her role as Viola in the collection by Russell Jackson and Robert Smallwood, *Players of Shakespeare 2* (1988), and Michael Pennington draws on his experience of directing the play for his detailed *Twelfth Night: A User's Guide* (2000). Michael Billington talks to directors in his *Directors' Shakespeare: Approaches to Twelfth Night* (1990) and Lois Potter considers four productions of the play in *Twelfth Night: Text and Performance* (1985). More recently, Emma Fielding discusses her role as Viola in the *Actors on Shakespeare* series (2002).

TWELFTH NIGHT AS UTOPIA

A book which is also highly recommended is Kiernan Ryan's *Shakespeare's Comedies* (2009). Ryan's chapter on *Twelfth Night* is an exuberant, illuminating and eminently readable discussion of the play as an examination of the self and a utopian and vulnerable vision of desire.

CHECK THE FILM **A03**

In the 1980 BBC TV production the actors performed to great effect in an intimate, naturalistic style suitable for the close-ups of television, with the result that audience sympathies were engaged in surprising and subtle ways, particularly with Malvolio. Why is the portrayal of Malvolio critical to the balance of comedy and **pathos** in the play?

CHECK THE BOOK **A03**

One of the most accessible recent discussions of Shakespeare's comedies is Michael Mangan's *A Preface to Shakespeare's Comedies 1594–1603* (1996). Mangan discusses comedy as structure and as humour, with reference to the contemporary context of the plays' performance, and then offers a series of detailed and stimulating readings of specific plays, including *Twelfth Night*.

PART SIX: GRADE BOOSTER

ASSESSMENT FOCUS

WHAT ARE YOU BEING ASKED TO FOCUS ON?

The questions or tasks you are set will be based around the four **Assessment Objectives**, **AO1** to **AO4**.

You may get more marks for certain **AOs** than others depending on which unit you're working on. Check with your teacher if you are unsure.

WHAT DO THESE AOS ACTUALLY MEAN?

ASSESSMENT OBJECTIVES	MEANING?
AO1 Articulate creative, informed and relevant responses to literary texts, using appropriate terminology and concepts, and coherent, accurate written expression.	You write about texts in accurate, clear and precise ways so that what you have to say is clear to the marker. You use literary terms (e.g. **apostrophe**) or refer to concepts (e.g. **irony**) in relevant places.
AO2 Demonstrate detailed critical understanding in analysing the ways in which structure, form and language shape meanings in literary texts.	You show that you understand the specific techniques and methods used by the writer(s) to create the text (e.g. **imagery**, **soliloquy**, etc.). You can explain clearly how these methods affect the meaning.
AO3 Explore connections and comparisons between different literary texts, informed by interpretations of other readers.	You are able to see relevant links between different texts. You are able to comment on how others (such as critics) view the text.
AO4 Demonstrate understanding of the significance and influence of the contexts in which literary texts are written and received.	You can explain how social, historical, political or personal backgrounds to the texts affected the writer and how the texts were read when they were first published and at different times since.

WHAT DOES THIS MEAN FOR YOUR REVISION?

Depending on the course you are following, you could be asked to:

- Respond to a general question about the text as a whole. For example:

How does Shakespeare use the idea of madness in *Twelfth Night* to create comic mayhem in Illyria?

- Write about an aspect of *Twelfth Night* which is also a feature of other texts you are studying. These questions may take the form of a challenging statement or quotation which you are invited to discuss. For example:

How far do you agree that comedy's prime concern is to reassure the audience and ultimately to reaffirm social norms?

- Or you may have to focus on the particular similarities, links, contrasts and differences between this text and others. For example:

Compare the ways Shakespeare uses the conventions of romantic comedy in *Twelfth Night* with the other text(s) you are studying.

EXAMINER'S TIP

Make sure you know how many marks are available for each **AO** in the task you are set. This can help you divide up your time or decide how much attention to give each aspect.

TARGETING A HIGH GRADE

It is very important to understand the progression from a lower grade to a high grade. In all cases, it is not enough simply to mention some key points and references – instead, you should explore them in depth, drawing out what is interesting and relevant to the question or issue.

TYPICAL C GRADE FEATURES

FEATURES	EXAMPLES
A01 You use critical vocabulary accurately, and your arguments make sense, are relevant and focus on the task. You show detailed knowledge of the text.	The opening lines of "Twelfth Night" show Shakespeare's use of the conventions of love poetry, including alliteration, apostrophe and paradox, to convey Orsino's self-indulgent love of being in love: 'If music be the food of love, play on;/ Give me excess of it, that surfeiting,/ The appetite may sicken and so die' (I.1.1–3).
A02 You can say how some specific aspects of form, structure and language shape meanings.	In "Twelfth Night", Shakespeare contrasts scenes for dramatic and comic effects. For example, Act II Scene 3, which ends with Orsino deciding to continue his wooing of Olivia, is immediately followed by Malvolio fantasising about marrying the Countess and being tricked into thinking she is in love with him.
A03 You consider, in detail, the connections between texts, and also how interpretations of texts differ, with some relevant supporting references.	In Shakespeare's earlier comedy, "As You Like It", Rosalind disguises herself as a man, but she appears as herself in women's clothing when she first meets her love Orlando. Viola, by contrast, never reappears in 'woman's weeds'. Consequently, the conventional ending of marriage in "As You Like It" is put off until later in "Twelfth Night" and instead we have the flirtation between Orsino and Cesario, and Orsino says, 'Cesario, come –/ For so you shall be while you are a man' (V.1.362–3).
A04 You can write about a range of contextual factors and make some specific and detailed links between these and the task or text.	Twelfth Night, like other Elizabethan festivals, involved normal relationships being turned upside down. Sometimes such festivals involved servants being waited on by their masters, or men wearing women's clothes or being ruled by their wives – Orsino's description of Cesario as her 'master's mistress' (V.1.304) and Viola's adoption of male clothing can be seen in this festival context.

TYPICAL FEATURES OF AN A OR A* RESPONSE

FEATURES	EXAMPLES
A01 You use appropriate critical vocabulary and a technically fluent style. Your arguments are well structured, coherent and always relevant, with a sharp focus on task.	With his declaration of love which opens the play, 'If music be the food of love, play on' (I.1.1), Orsino is established as an extravagant lover, indulging his hyperbolic passion for a woman who has made it clear she does not want anything to do with him. He does not seem to know Olivia as an individual, but his language is full of romantic clichés and preoccupied with the exquisite masochism of unrequited love: 'my desires, like fell and cruel hounds/ E'er since pursue me' (I.1.22–3).
A02 You explore and analyse key aspects of form, structure and language and evaluate perceptively how they shape meanings.	In "Twelfth Night", Shakespeare places scenes carefully in sequence, often juxtaposing them to create dramatic irony and also to maintain the comic tone. So, for instance, the scene in which Viola realises that Olivia has fallen in love with her is immediately preceded by the appearance of Sebastian, allowing the audience to enjoy Viola's predicament in the knowledge that there is a solution.
A03 You show a detailed and perceptive understanding of issues raised through connections between texts and can consider different interpretations with a sharp evaluation of their strengths and weaknesses. You use excellent supportive references.	In his closing remarks Orsino still addresses Viola as Cesario and comments on her 'masculine usurped attire' (V.1.234). Other of Shakespeare's cross-dressed heroines such as Rosalind in "As You Like It" or Portia in "The Merchant of Venice" re-establish their femininity at the end of the play by returning in their female clothes. In refusing to re-admit a feminine Viola, the play appears reluctant to relinquish the social and sexual topsy-turvy of carnival and misrule which it has portrayed.
A04 You show deep, detailed and relevant understanding(s) of how contextual factors link to the text or task.	In suggesting that Malvolio is a 'puritan' (II.3.119), Maria evokes the religious austerity of extreme Protestants or, as they were coming to be known, Puritans. When the Puritans came to power after the Civil War, one of their first acts in 1642 was to shut all the theatres. Sir Toby's 'cakes and ale' (II.3.98–9) riposte to Malvolio might be judged as a plea for a way of life which includes the theatre itself.

HOW TO WRITE HIGH-QUALITY RESPONSES

The quality of your writing – how you express your ideas – is vital for getting a higher grade, and **AO1** and **AO2** are specifically about **how** you respond.

FIVE KEY AREAS

The quality of your responses can be broken down into **five** key areas.

1. THE STRUCTURE OF YOUR ANSWER/ESSAY

- First, get **straight to the point in your opening paragraph**. Use a sharp, direct first sentence that deals with a key aspect and then follows up with evidence or a detailed reference.
- **Put forward an argument or point of view** (you won't always be able to challenge or take issue with the essay question, but generally, where you can, you are more likely to write in an interesting way).
- **Signpost your ideas** with connectives and references, which help the essay flow.
- **Don't repeat points already made**, not even in the conclusion, unless you have something new to say that adds a further dimension.

TARGETING A HIGH GRADE   A01

Here's an example of an opening paragraph that gets straight to the point, addressing the question:

'In _"Twelfth Night"_ music is not simply an accompaniment to the action, but an essential means of creating the play's bitter-sweet nature.' How do you respond to this viewpoint?

Immediate focus on task and key words, and example from text

Music begins, ends and permeates "Twelfth Night". Orsino's opening words, 'If music be the food of love, play on' (I.1.1), call for music not merely as entertainment, but as a prime physical need. Indeed, music encompasses and conveys the play's rich and complex pattern of moods, creating through its performance a mixture of sadness and joy which is one of the play's distinctive features.

2. USE OF TITLES, NAMES, ETC.

This is a simple, but important, tip to stay on the right side of the examiners.

- Make sure that you spell correctly the titles of the texts, characters, names of authors and so on. Present them correctly, too, with double quotation marks and capitals as appropriate. For example, '_In Act I of "Twelfth Night" ..._'.
- Use the **full title**, unless there is a good reason not to (e.g. it's very long).
- Use the terms 'play' or 'text' rather than 'book' or 'story'. If you use the word 'story', the examiner may think you mean the plot/action rather than the 'text' as a whole.

EXAMINER'S TIP ✓

Answer the question set, not the question you'd like to have been asked. Examiners say that often students will be set a question on one character (for example, Orsino) but end up writing almost as much about another (such as Malvolio). Or, they write about one aspect from the question (for example, 'disguise') but ignore another (such as 'gender identity'). **Stick to the question**, and answer **all parts of it**.

3. EFFECTIVE QUOTATIONS

Do not 'bolt on' quotations to the points you make. You will get some marks for including them, but examiners will not find your writing very fluent.

The best quotations are:

- Relevant
- Not too long
- Integrated into your argument/sentence.

TARGETING A HIGH GRADE   A01

Here is an example of a quotation successfully embedded in a sentence:

The more sombre tone of the play's denouement culminates in Orsino's final words, as he evokes a 'solemn combination … of our dear souls' (V.1.360–1).

Remember – quotations can be a well-selected set of three or four single words or phrases. These can be easily embedded into a sentence to build a picture or explanation around your point. Or, they can be longer quotations that are explored and picked apart.

> **GRADE BOOSTER   A02**
>
> It is important to remember that *Twelfth Night* is a text created by Shakespeare. Thinking about the voices Shakespeare makes with language and plotting will not only alert you to his methods as a playwright, but also his intentions, i.e. the effect he seeks to create.

4. TECHNIQUES AND TERMINOLOGY

By all means mention literary terms, techniques, conventions or people (for example, **rhetoric** or **eulogy** or 'Hazlitt') **but** make sure that you:

- Understand what they mean
- Are able to link them to what you're saying
- Spell them correctly.

5. GENERAL WRITING SKILLS

Try to write in a way that sounds professional and uses standard English. This does not mean that your writing will lack personality – just that it will be authoritative.

- Avoid colloquial or everyday expressions such as 'got', 'alright', 'ok' and so on.
- Use terms such as 'convey', 'suggest', 'imply', 'infer' to explain the writer's methods.
- Refer to 'we' when discussing the audience/reader.
- Avoid assertions and generalisations; don't just state a general point of view ('*Malvolio deserves everything he gets because he is vain and vindictive.*'), but analyse closely, with clear evidence and textual detail.

TARGETING A HIGH GRADE   A01

Note the professional approach in this example:

The imprisonment of Malvolio brings out the latent cruelty inherent in comedy. Nevertheless, while other characters progress beyond their self-delusions towards love of another, Malvolio goes the opposite way. Orsino escapes being 'canopied with bowers' (I.1.41) and Olivia from being a 'cloistress' (I.1.28), but Malvolio's 'self-love' (I.5.73), immediately identified by Olivia, leads him from his self-confinement in yellow stockings and cross-garters to his dungeon of isolation and darkness and finally to his exit from comedy itself, with his threat, 'I'll be revenged on the whole pack of you!' (V.1.355).

QUESTIONS WITH STATEMENTS, QUOTATIONS OR VIEWPOINTS

One type of question you may come across includes a statement, quotation or viewpoint. These questions ask you to respond to, or argue for/against, a specific point of view or critical interpretation.

For *Twelfth Night* these questions will typically be like this:

> ● **Discuss the view that Malvolio is a character who ultimately deserves pity rather than mockery.**
>
> ● **How far do you agree with Hazlitt's view that in *Twelfth Night* Viola is the 'great and secret charm' of the play?**
>
> ● **To what extent do you agree that in *Twelfth Night* Shakespeare demonstrates that being foolish is part of being human?**
>
> ● **Discuss the view that comic literature is subversive and undermines normal moral and social codes.**

The key thing to remember is that you are being asked to **respond to a critical interpretation** of the text – in other words, to come up with **your own** 'take' on the idea or viewpoint in the task.

KEY SKILLS REQUIRED

The table below provides help and advice on answering the question: **Discuss the view that Malvolio is a character who ultimately deserves pity rather than mockery.**

SKILL	WHAT DOES THIS MEAN?	HOW DO I ACHIEVE THIS?
Consider different interpretations	There will be more than one way of looking at the given question. For example, critics might be divided about the extent to which Malvolio is deserving of pity or mockery.	● Show you have considered these different interpretations in your answer. For example: *An unsympathetic interpretation would see Malvolio as a killjoy and 'party-pooper', a man who enjoys his moral superiority over his social superiors. If Malvolio is seen in a more positive light, however, we might think that he is only doing his job as the conscientious steward of a household that is still in mourning.*
Write with a clear, personal voice	Your own 'take' on the question is made obvious to the marker. You are not just repeating other people's ideas, but offering what **you** think.	● Although you may mention different perspectives on the task, you settle on your own view. ● Use language that shows careful, but confident, consideration. For example: *Although it has been said that … I feel that …*
Construct a coherent argument	The examiner or marker can follow your train of thought so that your own viewpoint is clear to him or her.	● Write in clear paragraphs that deal logically with different aspects of the question. ● Support what you say with well-selected and relevant evidence. ● Use a range of connectives to help 'signpost' your argument. For example: *Certainly Malvolio is thoroughly punished. While he is not alone in 'self-love' (I.5.73), he is disciplined and humiliated for this failing, unlike Orsino and Olivia, who are educated out of it through love. His name, however, Malvolio (mal = ill; volio = will) indicates his place in the comic scheme.*

ANSWERING A 'VIEWPOINT' QUESTION

Here is an example of a typical question on *Twelfth Night*:

> **Discuss the view that *Twelfth Night* is the most challenging of Shakespeare's comedies to produce because of the need to balance the 'sad and merry madness'.**

STAGE 1: DECODE THE QUESTION

Underline/highlight the **key words**, and make sure you understand what the statement, quotation or viewpoint is saying. In this case:

Key words = Discuss/challenging/produce/sad/merry/madness

The viewpoint/idea expressed is = in the performance of *Twelfth Night* there should be an interplay of comic and darker elements, laughter and melancholy

STAGE 2: DECIDE WHAT YOUR VIEWPOINT IS

Examiners have stated that they tend to reward a strong view which is clearly put. Think about the question – can you take issue with it? Disagreeing strongly can lead to higher marks, provided you have **genuine evidence** to support your point of view. Don't disagree just for the sake of it.

STAGE 3: DECIDE HOW TO STRUCTURE YOUR ANSWER

Pick out the key points you wish to make, and decide on the order in which you will present them. Keep this basic plan to hand while you write your response.

STAGE 4: WRITE YOUR RESPONSE

You could start by expanding on the statement or viewpoint expressed in the question.

● For example, in **Paragraph 1**:

"Twelfth Night" contains a complex pattern of moods and feelings, from the romantic posturing of Orsino to the drunken revelling of Sir Toby and his companions and the tense erotic interchanges between Olivia and Cesario.

This could help by setting up the various ideas you will choose to explore, argue for/against, and so on. But do not just repeat what the question says or just say what you are going to do. Get straight to the point. For example:

The play continues to have an impact because of the way the different elements are expressed through Shakespeare's characters, and also through the enduring relevance of issues concerning gender, identity and love …

Then, proceed to set out the different arguments or critical perspectives, including your own. This might be done by dealing with specific aspects or elements of the play, one by one. Consider giving 1–2 paragraphs to explore each aspect in turn. Discuss the strengths and weaknesses in each particular point of view. For example:

● **Paragraph 2**: first aspect:

*To answer whether this interpretation is valid, we need to **first of all** look at …*

*It is clear from this that… /a **strength** of this argument is …*

*However, I believe this suggests that …/a **weakness** in this argument is …*

● **Paragraph 3**: a new focus or aspect:

Turning our attention to the critical idea that *… it could be said that …*

● **Paragraphs 4, 5, etc. onwards**: develop the argument, building a convincing set of points:

Furthermore, if we look at …

● **Last paragraph**: end with a clear statement of your view, without simply listing all the points you have made:

*To say that the play appears more challenging to present because of its mixture of light and dark elements is only partly true, as **I believe that** …*

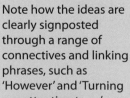

EXAMINER'S TIP ✓

You should comment concisely, professionally and thoughtfully and present a range of viewpoints. Try using modal verbs such as 'could', 'might', 'may' to clarify your own interpretation. For additional help on **Using critical interpretations and perspectives**, see pages 98 and 99.

EXAMINER'S TIP ✓

Note how the ideas are clearly signposted through a range of connectives and linking phrases, such as 'However' and 'Turning our attention to …'.

COMPARING *TWELFTH NIGHT* WITH OTHER TEXTS

As part of your assessment, you may have to compare *Twelfth Night* with, or link it to, other texts that you have studied. These may be other plays, novels or even poetry. You may also have to link or draw in references from texts written by critics. For example:

> **Compare the dramatic presentation of disguise and deception in** *Twelfth Night* **and other text(s) you have studied.**

THE TASK

Your task is likely to be on a method, issue, viewpoint or key aspect that is common to *Twelfth Night* and the other text(s), so you will need to:

Evaluate the issue or statement and have an **open-minded approach**. The best answers suggest meanings and interpretations (plural):

- What do you understand by the question? Is this theme more important in one text than in another? Why? How?
- What are the different ways that this question or aspect can be read or viewed?
- Can you challenge the viewpoint, if there is one? If so, what evidence is there? How can you present it in a thoughtful, reflective way?

Express original or creative approaches fluently:

- This isn't about coming up with entirely new ideas, but you need to show that you're actively engaged with thinking about the question and are not just reproducing random facts and information you have learned.
- **Synthesise** your ideas – pull ideas and points together to create something fresh.
- This is a linking/comparison response, so ensure that you guide your reader through your ideas logically, clearly and with professional language.

Know what to compare/contrast: form, structure and **language** will **always** be central to your response, even where you also have to write about characters, contexts or culture.

- Think about standard versus more conventional narration – for example, use of **juxtaposition**, **foreshadowing**, **dramatic irony**, disrupted time or narrative voice which leads to dislocation or questions in reading.
- Consider different characteristic use of language – length of lines, sentences, formal/informal style, dialect, accent, balance of dialogue and narration; the difference between forms, if appropriate (for example, prose treatment of an idea and a play) or the different ways two plays use the possibilities offered by drama.
- Look at a variety of **symbols**, **images**, **motifs** – how they represent concerns of author/time; what they are and how and where they appear; how they link to critical perspectives; their purposes, effects and impact on the play.
- Consider aspects of genres – to what extent do Shakespeare and the author(s) of the other work(s) conform to/challenge/subvert particular genres or styles of writing?

WRITING YOUR RESPONSE

The depth and extent of your answer will depend on how much you have to write, but the key will be to **explore in detail**, and **link between ideas and texts**. Let us use the example from page 94:

> Compare the dramatic presentation of disguise and deception in *Twelfth Night* and other text(s) you have studied.

INTRODUCTION TO YOUR RESPONSE

- Briefly discuss what 'disguise' and 'deception' mean, and how they apply to your texts.
- Mention the importance of disguise and deception in *Twelfth Night* and the other text(s).
- You could begin with a powerful quotation to launch into your response, for example:

> *'I am not what I am!' (III.1.126), Viola exclaims, as she tries to keep Olivia at bay, but her words only incite the Countess to declare her love. Viola's disguise, which she calls 'a wickedness' (II.2.24), affects all of the characters in Illyria, turning it into a topsy-turvy world of sexual carnival where the norm becomes not what you should, but 'what you will'.*

MAIN BODY OF YOUR RESPONSE

- **Point 1**: start with the dramatic presentation of disguise and deception in *Twelfth Night* and what they tell us about the play's concerns. What is your view? Are the uses of deception and disguise similar in the other text(s)? Are there any relevant critical viewpoints that you know about? Are there contextual or cultural factors to consider?

- **Point 2**: now cover a new treatment or aspect through comparison or contrast of this theme in your other text(s). How is this treatment or aspect presented **differently or similarly** by the writer(s) in the language, form, structures used? Why was this done in this way? How does it reflect the writer's interests? What do the critics say? Are there contextual or cultural factors to consider?

- **Points 3, 4, 5, etc.**: address a range of other factors and aspects, for example the disguise and deception of characters apart from the protagonists **either** within *Twelfth Night* **or** in both *Twelfth Night* and another text. What different ways do you respond to these (with more empathy, greater criticism, less interest) – and why? For example:

> *Viola declares 'I am not that I play' (I.5.153), but all of the main characters in "Twelfth Night" take on masks, assume postures and perform roles, from Orsino the romantic lover to 'Count' Malvolio, from Sir Andrew the duellist to Feste the jester, whose role as 'allowed' Fool (I.5.76) is itself a mask. The imagery, here and elsewhere, is not simply a reference to Viola's disguise, but is a teasing reminder that we are watching a play and so we too are implicated in the playing of roles.*

CONCLUSION

- Synthesise elements of what you have said into a final paragraph that fluently, succinctly and inventively leaves the reader/examiner with the sense that you have engaged with this task and the texts. For example:

> *Both Marlowe and Shakespeare have created dramatic worlds in which much is not what it seems. In Faustus, the audience is presented with a central character of great abilities who only realises the extent of the deception – which is really self-deception – at the moment of death, whereas in "Twelfth Night" Viola's disguise is redemptive, ironically leading Orsino and Olivia away from their confinement in self-deception to a 'solemn combination of dear souls' and loving union with another.*

EXAMINER'S TIP ✓

Be creative with your conclusion! It's the last thing the examiner will read and your chance to make your mark.

EXAMINER'S TIP ✓

You may be asked to discuss other texts you have studied as well as *Twelfth Night* as part of your response, for example *King Lear*. Once you have completed your response on the play you could move on to discuss the same issues in your other text(s). Begin with a simple linking phrase or sentence to launch straight into your first point about your next text, such as: '*The same issue/idea is explored in quite a different way in [name of text]. Here …*'.

RESPONDING TO A GENERAL QUESTION ABOUT THE WHOLE TEXT

You may also be asked to write about a specific aspect of *Twelfth Night* – but as it relates to the **whole text**. For example:

> **Explore the dramatic use Shakespeare makes of the Fool and folly in *Twelfth Night*.**

This means you should:

- Focus on *both* **the figure of the Fool** *and* **the foolishness and folly of different characters**.
- **Explain their 'dramatic use' in comedy and tragedy**. Compare and contrast how they are used by Shakespeare in terms of action, character and furthering ideas or themes. Consider the dramatic conventions linked to them. With the Fool these include jokes and the slipperiness of language, catechising, songs and a **choric** role. Folly in *Twelfth Night* is linked to the dramatic conventions of comedy, including wordplay, mistakes, disguise, confusions and tricks, which come together in the 'gulling' of Malvolio.
- Look at aspects of the **whole play text**, not just one scene.

STRUCTURING YOUR RESPONSE

You need a clear, logical plan, as for all tasks that you do. It is impossible to write about every section or part of the text, so you will need to:

- Quickly note 5–6 key points or aspects to build your essay around, such as:

  Point a *Feste, like Lear's Fool, mediates truth and has a choric role.*
  Point b *The role of the fool in "Twelfth Night" is linked to the dramatic conventions of comedy and tragedy in the play, which come together in the gulling of Malvolio.*
  Point c *Music has a particular importance in the role of Feste – see Feste's valedictory song.*
  Point d *The violence and madness in the play can be seen as a kind of foolishness and bring about a variety of effects from comedy and horror to mirth and pathos.*
  Point e *Shakespeare links foolery with disguise and theatricality to draw attention to the masks we wear every day.*

- Then decide the most effective or logical order. For example, **point d**, then **a, e, c, b**, etc.

You could begin with your key or main idea, with supporting evidence/references, followed by your further points (perhaps two paragraphs for each). For example:

Paragraph 1: first key point. *"Twelfth Night" is a comedy whose delight is informed by dark elements.*

Paragraph 2: expand out, link into other areas. *Feste's catechising and wordplay always leave him in control. When Malvolio asserts 'I am as well in my wits, fool, as thou art', Feste responds, 'But as well? Then you are mad indeed, if you be no better in your wits than a fool' (IV.2.73–6).*

Paragraph 3: change direction, introduce new aspect/point. *The comic business in Illyria arises from the theatrical trick of Viola's disguise, which she calls a 'wickedness' (II.2.24), and she frequently draws attention to her role as actor: 'I would be loath to cast away my speech: for besides that it is excellently well penned, I have taken great pains to con it' (I.5.142–4). And so on.*

Use a compelling way to finish, perhaps repeating some or all of the key words from the question. For example, you could end with your final point, but **add a last clause** which makes it clear what you think is key to the question: e.g. *Mixing tragic and comic elements in "Twelfth Night" enables Shakespeare to create and intensify dramatic effects on stage and add to the exploration of the genres, through both language and action.*

EXAMINER'S TIP ✓

You could end with a **new quotation or an aspect that's slightly different from** your main point: e.g. *The final words of King Lear's Fool, determining to 'go to bed at noon' (III.6.83), leave us with the idea of a mysterious presence whose utterances have a disturbing and dark profundity. In contrast, Feste is a wise fool who moves through the play, rootless and aloof, and we laugh and feel sad with him.*

WRITING ABOUT CONTEXTS

Assessment Objective 4 asks you to 'demonstrate understanding of the significance and influence of the contexts in which literary texts are written and received ...'. This can mean:

● How the events, settings, politics and so on **of the time when the text was written** influenced the writer or help us to understand the play's themes or concerns. For example, to what extent Shakespeare might have been influenced by arguments about religion in Elizabethan England.

or

● How events, settings, politics and so on **of the time when the text is read or seen** influence how it is understood. For example, would audiences watching the play today see parallels between Viola's disguise and modern questions of gender roles, sexuality and identity?

THE CONTEXT FOR *TWELFTH NIGHT*

You might find the following table of suggested examples helpful for thinking about how particular aspects of the time contribute to our understanding of the play and its themes. These are just examples – can you think of any others?

POLITICAL	LITERARY	PHILOSOPHICAL
The Elizabethan age Machiavelli and *The Prince*	Plautus, *Menaechmi* Italian drama *Gl'Ingannati* University wits and playwrights, Marlowe, Kyd, Lyly **Sonnets** and love poetry **Rhetoric** Sir Philip Sidney and Edmund Spenser	Plato Pythagoras Humanism

SCIENTIFIC	CULTURAL	SOCIAL
Discoveries in astronomy, exploration and new maps	The Renaissance Music and songs Christmas and Epiphany	Puritanism

TARGETING A HIGH GRADE

Remember that the extent to which you write about these contexts will be determined by the marks available. Some questions or tasks may have very few marks allocated for **AO4**, but where you do have to refer to context the key thing is **not** to 'bolt on' your comments, or write a long, separate chunk of text on context and then 'go back' to the play. For example:

Don't just write:

The late sixteenth century was a time of religious ferment in England. Under the young King Edward VI, many Catholic rituals were abolished, only to be restored when Mary became Queen in 1553. During Mary's reign, almost 300 Protestants were burnt at the stake for their beliefs; when her half-sister Elizabeth succeeded her in 1558, Catholics were oppressed and priests executed, especially when Mary's husband, Philip II of Spain, declared war on England in 1588. The reign of Elizabeth I saw the rise of the Puritans, who advocated an extreme form of Protestantism.

Do write:

Shakespeare's audiences would have found echoes of religious controversies of their time through the play, particularly in relation to Malvolio. In suggesting that Malvolio is a 'puritan' (II.3.119), Maria evokes a context of religious austerity, as practised by extreme Protestants or, as they were coming to be known, Puritans. But there is also a political significance too to the 'gulling' of Malvolio. The Puritans proposed a form of democracy which would have power over the sovereign and so Malvolio's grotesque humiliation could also be seen as a means of attacking as morally hypocritical a movement which was a social and political threat to the order of the day.

> **EXAMINER'S TIP** ✓
>
> Remember that linking the historical, literary or social context to the play is key to achieving the best marks for **AO4**.

USING CRITICAL INTERPRETATIONS AND PERSPECTIVES

THE 'MEANING' OF A TEXT

There are many viewpoints and perspectives on the 'meaning' of *Twelfth Night*, and examiners will be looking for evidence that you have considered a range of these. Broadly speaking, these different interpretations might relate to the following considerations.

1. CHARACTER

What **sort/type** of person Orsino – or another character – is:

- Is the character an **archetype** (a specific type of character with common features)? Orsino adopts the role of romantic lover, who luxuriates in his love of being in love. In this he is reminiscent of the classical figure of Narcissus and other similar figures.

- Does the character personify, **symbolise** or represent a specific idea or **trope** (self-obsession, sexism and a petulant egotism, where love is seen as a means of self-gratification and glorification ('one self king'), etc.)?

- Is the character modern, universal, of his/her time, historically accurate, etc.? Can we see aspects of Orsino's vanity, sexual fantasising, fickleness and fretful posturing in public figures (such as actors or pop idols, intellectuals or politicians) from our own time?

2. IDEAS AND ISSUES

What the play tells us about **particular ideas or issues** and how we can interpret these. For example:

- The nature of love

- Questions of identity and the self

- Sexuality, desire and the body

- Moral and social codes.

3. LINKS AND CONNECTIONS

To what extent the play **links with, follows or pre-echoes** other texts and/or ideas. For example:

- Its influence culturally, historically and socially. Do we see echoes of the characters or genres in other texts? How like Viola are other cross-dressed heroines, such as Margery Pinchwife in Wycherley's *The Country Wife*, Hellena in *The Rover* by Aphra Behn, or Nan Astley in *Tipping the Velvet* by Sarah Waters, or female characters who remain silent about their love, such as Jane Eyre? Does the play share features with Morality Plays?

- How its language links to other texts or modes, such as religious works, myth, tales, etc.

4. DRAMATIC STRUCTURE

How the play is **constructed** and how Shakespeare **makes** his narrative:

- Does it follow particular dramatic conventions?

- What is the function of specific events, characters, theatrical devices, staging, etc. in relation to narrative?

- What are the specific moments of tension, conflict, crisis and denouement – and do we agree on what they are?

CRITICAL VIEWPOINT **A03**

In *Shakespeare's Festive Comedy* (1959), C. L. Barber writes: 'The most fundamental distinction the play brings home to us is the difference between men and women ... Just as ... reversal of social roles need not threaten the social structure, but can serve to consolidate it, so a temporary, playful reversal of sexual roles can renew the meaning of the normal relation.'

5. AUDIENCE RESPONSE

How the play **works on an audience**, and whether this changes over time and in different contexts:

● Are we to empathise with, feel distance from, judge and/or evaluate the events and characters?

6. CRITICAL REACTION

And, finally, how different audiences view the play: for example, different **theatre critics over time**, or different **audiences** in **earlier or more recent years**.

WRITING ABOUT CRITICAL PERSPECTIVES

The important thing to remember is that **you** are a critic too. Your job is to evaluate what a critic or school of criticism has said about the elements above, and arrive at your own conclusions.

In essence, you need to: **consider** the views of others, **synthesise** them, then decide on **your perspective**. For example:

EXPLAIN THE VIEWPOINTS

Critical view A about *Twelfth Night* and the permutations of romantic love

> *C. L. Barber argues that "Twelfth Night" inverts sexual and gender roles ultimately to re-establish and confirm normal relations.*

Critical view B about *Twelfth Night* and the permutations of romantic love

> *Other critics argue that the energy of the play subverts rather than confirms traditional values, avoiding fixing gender identity and desire in a conventional romantic ending, and instead preferring to postpone marriage until 'golden time convents' (V.1.359).*

THEN SYNTHESISE AND ADD YOUR PERSPECTIVE

Synthesising these views whilst adding your own:

> *Sebastian could be seen as a physical solution to the play's sexual dilemmas and one which is provided reassuringly soon by Shakespeare so that the audience is secure in the knowledge that sexual order will be restored through the final romantic pairings. Barber also invokes the compelling cultural precedent of festivals, which act as a safety-valve for rebellion, leaving the status quo intact. For Kott, however, Sebastian makes no difference since Viola is Cesario is Sebastian, or, as Orsino says, 'One face, one voice, one habit, and two persons' (V.1.200). Seen in this light, the final pairings are more complex and the ambiguity in gender remains in play, Olivia being 'betrothed both to a maid and man' (V.1.247) and Orsino's page becoming his 'master's mistress' (V.1.304) but remaining in male clothes and being addressed as 'Cesario' (V.1.362) and 'man' (V.1.363).*
>
> *So in my view, desire, of Orsino for his page, of Olivia for a woman, and of Antonio for his young master, is not 'confined' in marriage resolutions, and the fact that the play was originally performed by an all-male cast only adds to the confusion which Shakespeare allows to reign.*

GRADE BOOSTER **A03**

Make sure you have thoroughly explored the dramatic conventions. Critical interpretation of drama is different from critical interpretation of other modes of writing – not least because of audience response, and the specific theatrical devices in use. Key critics are theatre critics – look at what they have to say about recent productions.

ANNOTATED SAMPLE ANSWERS

Below are extracts from two sample answers to the same question at different grades. Bear in mind that these are examples only, covering all four Assessment Objectives – you will need to check the type of question and the weightings given for the four Assessment Objectives when writing your coursework essay or practising for your exam.

Question: **To what extent could it be said that *Twelfth Night* is a play in which true love is shown to be more powerful than self-love?**

The text below is part of a longer response of 1,200 words. The student has chosen to write about Orsino and Malvolio.

CANDIDATE 1

It is really clear from the play's ending that true love has come out on top with the coming marriages of Viola and Orsino, and Sebastian and Olivia. The self-loving Malvolio disappears from the stage and the audience is left with the happy picture of the two couples, 'dear souls', as Orsino refers to them (V.1).

AO1 Clear statement based on essay title but would be useful to explore relevance of true love in relation to the play as a whole

But I think that for much of the play the battle between the two ideas has been in the balance. 'Self-love' could be seen to be the more dominant of the two from the moment Orsino exaggerates his feelings for Olivia by demanding 'excess' of music to feed his emotions in Act I Scene 1. His words are sickly-sweet and do not ring true, even his pun when asked if he will go hunting 'the hart', and replies that, metaphorically, he already does – Olivia's – is rather pathetic and feels forced. For someone to spend so much time talking about love, rather than doing something about it suggests it is false. It reminds us of Romeo's words about Rosalind in "Romeo and Juliet" and implies that Shakespeare wishes to mock such self-deception. Orsino's final words of the first scene, 'Love-thoughts lie rich when canopied with bowers', make us think he is more in love with the idea of love, and what it makes you do, than actually 'in love' with Olivia. It is significant that the first line of the next scene is spoken by Viola and is direct and to the point, 'What country, friends, is this?', and is concerned with action and not just thinking.

AO2 Good understanding of literary device but further development needed

AO1 Could be expressed more fluently – what does 'in love' mean, in this context?

AO3 Excellent link to another work, but no reference and does not explore the idea sufficiently

AO2 Intelligent comment on language and its effect, but also undeveloped

Orsino's self-love can be seen even in his scenes with Viola/Cesario. You would think that once he was with her, even though he thinks she is a boy, his 'true love' would make him behave more truthfully. In fact he is even more boastful in Act II Scene 4. It is true that he admits men's feelings are 'more giddy and unfirm,/ More longing, wavering, sooner lost and worn,/ Than women's are' (II.4.31–3), but this does not lead him to realise how 'giddy' his love for Olivia is. In fact, he argues with Viola that women cannot feel passions as strongly as he does. 'Make no compare/ Between that love a woman can bear me,/ And that I owe Olivia' (II.4.97–100). The contrast between this, and Viola's simple, unspoken love for him and her painful feelings for her seemingly-dead brother are very striking.

AO1 Expression is a little simplistic here – is 'boastful' the right word?

AO2 Well-chosen quotation

AO1 Point is well-developed

AO1 Nicely drawn conclusion, expressed clearly

AO3 Good reference to alternative readings of the same idea, although rather undeveloped

Whether her speech about 'Patience on a monument' at the end of this scene gets through to him is something that is left open by Shakespeare. One possible meaning to his final lines, sending Viola off to take the jewel to Olivia, is that he remains just as absorbed by his 'false' love for her, but another could argue that in saying so little in response to the speech, he is indicating his changed feelings. You could say that silence is worth a million words.

When Orsino finally does get to see Olivia, his exaggerated praise has been reduced to a kind of throwaway comment: 'Here comes the countess; now heaven walks on earth' (V.1.86).

AO1 Well-made point, but expression is a little clumsy

AO1 Far too vague – express in a different way and refer to direct evidence

It is as if he has forgotten how to do all the flowery emotional stuff of earlier on in the play. Perhaps for once he is thinking less of himself and actually about someone else – Viola/Cesario. As has been pointed out by some critics, Orsino the hunter has become, without knowing it, the hunted. Having referred to himself as 'one self-same king' (I.1) who will rule Olivia's heart, by the end he talks like a Renaissance poet about Viola as his 'Fancy's Queen' suggesting she rules him. This reversal of fortune represents the way self-love is conquered by true love.

AO3 Fascinating point, but specific critic must be referenced

AO4 Appropriate reference to context here but idea needs to be much more developed

AO1 Clear summary of this idea

In Malvolio, however, self-love dominates from start to finish ...

(Here, the candidate moves on to discuss Malvolio in relation to the essay title.)

GRADE C

Comment

AO1 Some very good expression spoiled by occasional vague or sloppy turns of phrase. The argument is well-made and clear, if a little undeveloped in places. The question is largely addressed but an initial exploration of the nature of 'true' love and what that means, before exploring whether it can be said to dominate, would have helped.

AO2 Some useful and pertinent quotations, generally embedded fluently and one or two references to linguistic devices and their effects, although greater exploration of the 'hart' **motif** might have helped the argument. The candidate touches on ideas about contrasting language styles, as in the reference to Viola's first lines, but this is a little basic.

AO3 Some consideration of alternative interpretations or readings, but these relate more to the nature of Orsino's 'self-love' rather than critiquing the idea of 'self-love' itself. Critics must be referenced by name, if referred to.

AO4 Little in the way of contextual reference. Whether in exploring the conventions of romantic love poetry and what might be seen as 'truthful' or in understanding the impact role and gender reversals would have had on an audience's reading of 'love', both now and in Shakespeare's day, something in this area is required.

For a B grade

To gain a higher grade, the answer must include at least some of the following:

- More fluent expression and more detailed exploration of the key ideas
- Greater reference to contextual factors such as role and status in Elizabethan society
- More detailed reference to critics and alternative interpretations.

CANDIDATE 2

A01 Excellent exploration of key words from title

A01 Interesting, but this covers perhaps too much in one phrase

The fictional identity of the country whose name is the answer to shipwrecked Viola's first question – 'Illyria' – suggests that any exploration of what is 'true' must be taken with a large pinch of (sea) salt. How are we to judge 'true love'? We think of it as innate, growing from something natural and not forced, but it is quite a leap of faith for us to believe the idea that a man might love a woman dressed as a boy who is his servant. On the other hand, it might imply that true love conquers all bounds – gender, status and appearance. In this sense, it is easy to argue that Orsino's expressions of love for Olivia in Act 1 Scene 1, peppered as they are by a litany of words and phrases associated with disease such as 'excess', 'pestilence' and 'dying fall' have more in common with Malvolio, described as 'sick of self-love', than with anyone else.

A02 Excellent and relevant references leading to a key point

Yet, Orsino's extended metaphorical response to Curio's question of whether he will go hunting, is part of a convention of courtly and romantic love poetry well-established in earlier and contemporary verse, and could be seen to enhance his status as wretched lover. In the same way, Thomas Wyatt, in translating Petrarch, writes in his sonnet 'Whoso list to hunt' of his pursuit of a deer that is too wild to tame, a reference many claim to be to Anne Boleyn. Yet, while Wyatt's sonnet is enigmatic and mysterious, here Orsino tells Curio directly who he is describing, and while he suggests it is he who has become the pursued deer chased by his 'desires like cruel and fell hounds' the comparison is forced and unconvincing, driven perhaps by vanity rather than courtly convention.

A04 Useful reference to literary context

A04 Not sure this is relevant; needs further comment

A03 Excellent linking between texts

A02 Clear structural link to other points in the play

This self-love is equally evident in Orsino's other dialogues. Until the final denouement, he continues to play the role of spurned lover, safe in his court. For example, we observe his exchange with Viola/Cesario in Act 1 Scene 4 in which even the spontaneity of his expressions of love for Olivia are planned: 'Surprise her with discourse of my dear faith;/ It shall become thee well to act my woes' (1.4.24–5).

A04 Excellent interpretation and insight into the language and context although specific examples needed

A03 Helpful critical reference

While the idea of intermediaries between lovers is by no means unusual in Elizabethan society, the fact that Orsino instructs Cesario to 'surprise' Olivia and 'act' out his role, indicates a false basis to the love he professes. In contrast, Viola, subject to what John Wilders calls the 'motiveless, impersonal attacks of fate', behaves without much strategy, deciding 'on the spot' to disguise herself and see where things take her. There is arrogance therefore in Orsino's words, a feeling that a woman can be swayed by language and strategy, rather than raw direct emotion.

A02
Appropriate quotation fluently embedded into text

A01
Relevant literary device cited

This has by no means dissipated by Act II Scene 4 when Viola/Cesario seems to have momentarily caught the disease of hyperbole herself when talking about love. When asked about the melody being played, she replies, 'It gives a very echo to the seat/ Where love is throned.'

It is ironic that the woman who most personifies 'true' love in remaining silent about the Duke, and her seemingly-dead brother, is reduced to mimicking Orsino's false expressions. However, whilst Orsino proceeds to argue later in the scene that women cannot feel passion as strongly as he can, which is as 'hungry as the sea' (line 96), he himself is finally driven to a kind of silence by Viola's 'Patience on a monument' speech. He tamely ends the scene by sending Viola off with a jewel for Olivia – with no further flowery instructions to act out a role.

A02
Excellent connection, well expressed

A01
Fluent restating of the focus of the essay in one phrase

One could argue that at the final scene's conclusion Orsino has been taught how to love truthfully by Viola, whose own understanding of it has been hardened by experience. He has become the 'hart' of his first speech, although his desires have driven him in a different direction from the one he was seeking. Ironically, Orsino's final speech to Viola states that she will remain in role as Cesario, 'For so you shall be while you are a man' (V.1.363), suggesting that 'true love' ultimately arises out of 'false face', if not out of 'false' love. To that extent, true love has triumphed.

A02
Suggests an interesting and original angle on Orsino's affections and ends this section intelligently

(*Here, the candidate moves on to discuss other aspects of "Twelfth Night" in relation to the essay title.*)

GRADE A

Comment

A01 Expression throughout is sophisticated and informed, although in seeking to pursue original lines of debate the argument occasionally gets lost. 'False' and 'self' love may not be quite the same thing, and this needs further clarification.

A02 Excellent critical understanding of how language and structure affect meaning, especially in identifying key **tropes** or **motifs** such as the 'hart' and what it might imply.

A03 Different interpretations are clearly signposted, and critical comment fluently interwoven in the response, although the initial excellent reading of what 'true' love might be is not perhaps pursued to its logical conclusion in questioning whether Orsino replaces one fantasy (Olivia) with another (Cesario/Viola).

A04 This is particularly strong in the response; in referencing Wyatt and the motif of the 'hart', as well as the conventions of courtly and romantic love poetry, the student demonstrates how our understanding of the intention of love poetry can lead us either to question Orsino's sincerity, or applaud it.

For an A* grade

- Clarify the argument and follow it through with unwavering attention to the key focuses. Simplify the opening paragraph without losing the insight and original thinking.

- Cut out unnecessary contextual reference unless genuinely informing the argument.

- Don't try to cover too many aspects within one sentence or paragraph, but unpack each idea clearly and carefully for the reader.

WORKING THROUGH A TASK

Now it's your turn to work through a task on *Twelfth Night*. The key is to:

- Read/decode the task/question.
- Plan your points – then expand and link your points.
- Draft your answer.

TASK TITLE

> 'Shakespeare's enthronement of woman as queen of comedy is no mere accident … these heroines have attributes of personality fitting them more certainly than men to shape the world toward happiness' (H. B. Charlton, *Shakespeare's Heroines and the Art of Happiness*). In your view how well does this statement apply to the female characters in *Twelfth Night*?

In your view…?	= what are **my** views?
comedy	= a reminder that this is a literary creation in a specific genre
attributes of personality	= discussion of the different aspects of the 'female characters'
heroines	= consider Viola in detail

PLAN AND EXPAND

- Key aspect: evidence of 'woman as queen of comedy'

POINT	EXPANDED POINT	EVIDENCE
Point a In "Twelfth Night" the female characters are active, prime movers in creating the comedy.	Viola's disguise is central to creating the comic confusion in Illyria. Maria's letter tricks Mavolio. Olivia's love for Cesario places them both in an urgent and intense 'comic' predicament. You could also argue that Feste is the professional joker and the other male characters could be seen as the butt of the comedy.	Quotations 1–2 Olivia: 'Are you a comedian?' Viola: 'No my profound heart; and yet, by the very fangs of malice, I swear, I am not that I play.' (I.5.151–3) Olivia: 'I am as mad as he/ If sad and merry madness equal be.' (III.4.14–15)
Point b The different 'attributes of personality' of the female characters help to produce different comic situations.	Different aspects of this point expanded *You fill in*	Quotations 1–2 *You fill in*
Point c Viola's role in the comedy is varied and central to the spirit of the play.	Different aspects of this point expanded *You fill in*	Quotations 1–2 *You fill in*

- Key aspect: evidence that the female characters 'shape' Illyria 'toward happiness'

POINT	EXPANDED POINT	EVIDENCE
Point a *You fill in*	Expanded: *You fill in*	Quotations 1–2 *You fill in*
Point b *You fill in*	Different aspects of this point expanded *You fill in*	Quotations 1–2 *You fill in*
Point c *You fill in*	Different aspects of this point expanded *You fill in*	Quotations 1–2 *You fill in*

CONCLUSION

POINT	EXPANDED POINT	EVIDENCE
Key final point or overall view *You fill in*	Draw together and perhaps add a final further point to support your view *You fill in*	Final quotation to support your view *You fill in*

DEVELOP FURTHER, THEN DRAFT

Now look back over your draft points and:

● Add further links or connections between the points to develop them further or synthesise what has been said, for example:

> *Commentators as varied as A. C. Bradley, Terry Eagleton and Kiernan Ryan have discussed the special role that Feste performs in the comedy, providing through his wit and ingenuity a philosophical, or more precisely 'foolosophical', perspective on events, ideas and language itself. His very aloofness is also a necessary limit on his participation in the comic business and revelry. Viola, however, engages in verbal fencing with Feste and also the mock fencing with Sir Andrew, and remains at the centre of the comedy as the source and focus of the mistakes and misapprehensions which cause the madness and mayhem in Illyria.*

● Decide an order for your points/paragraphs – some may now be linked/connected and therefore **not** in the order of the table above.

● Now draft your essay. If you're really stuck you can use the opening paragraph below to get you started.

> *The gulling of Malvolio was the comic device which the law student John Manningham noted in the earliest account of a performance of "Twelfth Night", and certainly the business with the cross-garters is a comic high point in the drama, but the trap was laid with ingenuity, wit and a sharp knowledge of the steward's weaknesses by a maidservant, the feisty Maria. Feste is the professional fool and Sir Andrew a natural one and along with Sir Toby their revelling provides great entertainment, but Maria, Olivia and Viola, the women and a woman as a boy, are the active and prime movers in generating the particular warmth, variety and spirit of the comedy in "Twelfth Night".*

Once you've written your essay, turn to page 112 for a mark scheme on this question to see how well you've done.

FURTHER QUESTIONS

1. 'Give me excess of it …' Discuss the theme of excess in *Twelfth Night*, and another play you have studied, and show how it relates to at least two of the characters and their conflicts in each play.

2. 'I am not what I am.' Discuss masking and role play in *Twelfth Night* in relation to the questions of gender identity and the nature of the self which the play raises.

3. How does 'sad and merry madness' turn the world of Illyria upside down and by extension challenge the accepted norms of the audience?

4. 'One face, one voice, one habit and two persons …' Show how Shakespeare uses the device of identical twins to create comic business, raise questions of identity and to provide a resolution to the drama in *Twelfth Night* and another text you have studied.

5. 'Ourselves we do not owe …' Consider the theme of chance and show how different characters react to the idea of fate in *Twelfth Night*.

6. 'Unrequited love, melancholy, cruelty and joy held in perfect balance.' Explain what you think Nicholas Hytner means in this statement about *Twelfth Night*.

7. From the opening lines the play's powerful imagery takes its effect. Explore two examples of threads of imagery which run through the play, for example the sea and flowers, and show how they enrich our understanding and experience of the characters, events and themes in the play.

8. The comedy in *Twelfth Night* becomes increasingly threatening and violent, culminating in Malvolio's threat of revenge which goes beyond laughter. Discuss these darker elements in the play and show how they contribute to the play's mood.

9. '*Twelfth Night* does not give us the happy ending that we might expect from a romantic comedy.' Evaluate this view with particular reference to the long final scene and Feste's valedictory song.

ESSENTIAL STUDY TOOLS

FURTHER READING

THE TEXT AND ITS SOURCE

E. S. Donno, ed., *Twelfth Night: The New Cambridge Shakespeare*, Introduction by Penny Gay, Cambridge University Press, 2004
The edition referred to in these Notes; includes an excellent introduction which addresses key themes, a detailed stage history and full explanatory notes

CRITICISM

The following books and essays tend to consider *Twelfth Night* as festive comedy and in terms of social myths and rituals:

C. L. Barber, *Shakespeare's Festive Comedy*, Princeton University Press, 1959

J. A. Bryant, *Shakespeare and the Uses of Comedy*, University of Kentucky, 1974

H. B. Charlton, *Shakespearian Comedy*, Routledge Kegan & Paul, 1938

L. Hotson, *The First Night of Twelfth Night*, Rupert Hart-Davis, 1954

D. J Palmer, ed., *Twelfth Night*, Casebook Series, Macmillan, 1972
See for example W. Hazlitt, *The Comedy of Nature*, pp. 29–36 (1817); H. Granville-Barker, *Twelfth Night an Acting Edition*, pp. 57–8 (1912); B. Evans, *The Fruits of the Sport*, pp. 137–69 (1960)

J. D. Wilson, *Shakespeare's Happy Comedies*, Faber & Faber, 1962

The following tend to see the comedy contending with darker elements or being unresolved to leave questions of language, desire, identity and gender:

D. Barker and I. Kamps, *Shakespeare and Gender: A History*, Verso, 1995

T. Eagleton, *William Shakespeare*, Basil Blackwell, 1986

J. M. Gregson, *Shakespeare, Twelfth Night*, Studies in English Literature No. 72, Edward Arnold, 1980

J. Kott, *Shakespeare Our Contemporary* (first published 1964), Norton, 1974

L. Jardine, *Still Harping on Daughters: Women and Drama in the Age of Shakespeare*, Columbia University Press, 2nd edn, 1989

M. Mangan, *A Preface to Shakespeare's Comedies 1594–1603*, Longman, 1996

S. Orgel, *Impersonations: The Performance of Gender in Shakespeare's England*, Cambridge University Press, 1996

K. Ryan, *Shakespeare's Comedies*, Palgrave Macmillan, 2009

V. Traub, *Desire and Anxiety: Circulations of Sexuality in Shakespearean Drama*, Routledge, 1992

R. S. White, ed., *Twelfth Night: Contemporary Critical Essays*, New Casebook, Macmillan, 1996

The following consider fundamental elements and features of Shakespeare's work:

J. Bate, *The Genius of Shakespeare*, Picador, 1997

J. Bate, *Shakespeare and Ovid*, Oxford University Press, 1993

J. Bate, *Soul of the Age*, Penguin, 2009

S. Greenblatt, *Will in the World*, Pimlico, 2005

F. Kermode, *Shakespeare's Language*, Penguin, 2000

C. Spurgeon, *Shakespeare's Imagery and What It Tells Us*, 1935

TWELFTH NIGHT IN PERFORMANCE

These books present the views and experiences of actors and directors of *Twelfth Night*:

M. Billington, *Directors' Shakespeare: Approaches to Twelfth Night*, Nick Hern Books, 1990

J. R. Brown, *The Routledge Companion to Directors' Shakespeare*, Routledge, 2008

E. Fielding, *Twelfth Night, Actors on Shakespeare*, Faber & Faber, 2002

R. Jackson and R. Smallwood, *Players of Shakespeare 2*, Cambridge University Press, 1988

M. Pennington, *Twelfth Night: A User's Guide*, Nick Hern Books, 2000

L. Potter, *Twelfth Night: Text and Performance*, Macmillan, 1985

FILM VERSIONS OF TWELFTH NIGHT

Twelfth Night, The Shakespeare Collection, BBC DVD, 1980, directed by John Gorrie with Alec McCowen as Malvolio, Felicity Kendall as Viola, Sinead Cusack as Olivia
This BBC TV production, in Elizabethan costume, is a faithful rendition of the text and an excellent use of the medium, subtly balancing humour and pathos in an intimate, naturalistic style. It is distinguished by excellent performances from the whole cast.

Twelfth Night, Renaissance Theatre Production for Channel 4 Television, 1988, directed by Kenneth Branagh with Kenneth Briers as Malvolio, Frances Barber as Viola and Caroline Langrishe as Olivia
The wintry TV studio setting captures an underlying melancholy and sense of the strangeness in Illyria. This beautifully acted production in a period (Victorian) setting interweaves the comedy with powerful moments of tenderness and pathos and is helped by music from Patrick Doyle and Sir Paul McCartney. The DVD also has an extra feature, 'Inside An Illyrian Winter', which is an illuminating 21-minute interview with Kenneth Branagh.

Twelfth Night, film directed by Trevor Nunn, 1996, with Nigel Hawthorne as Malvolio, Imogen Stubbs as Viola and Helena Bonham Carter as Olivia
The film has an Edwardian setting and was shot on the Cornish coast. The inventive direction provides a surprising and refreshing take on familiar scenes and the accomplished performances have a vibrant energy and wit which are always engaging. The film does make some significant changes to the play, however, adding a pseudo-Shakespearean narrative for a sequence on the boat before the shipwreck, changing the setting and order of scenes and showing a happy ending with Viola in 'woman's weeds', so it is worth ensuring that this is not the only production to be viewed.

Remember that the best way to experience *Twelfth Night* is at the theatre.

LITERARY TERMS

allegory   a story or a situation with two different meanings, where the straightforward meaning on the surface is used to **symbolise** a deeper meaning underneath

apostrophe   a **rhetorical** term for a speech addressed to a person or thing

archetype   a typical or representative figure of a particularly imposing kind

aside   dramatic convention by which a character on stage says something that the audience, but not all the other characters, can hear

bathos   a ludicrous descent from the elevated treatment of a subject to the ordinary and dull

blank verse   unrhymed lines of **iambic pentameter**

blazon   a poetic device in which the lover's eyes, lips, cheeks and hair are catalogued and separately described

caesura   a strong pause for sense and syntax, within a metrical line

carnival   a literary phenomenon described by the Russian critic Mikhail Bakhtin, especially in his work *Rabelais and his World* (1965). According to him some writers use their works as an outlet for the spirit of carnival, of popular festivity and *misrule*. They 'subvert' the literary culture of the ruling classes, undermining its claim to moral monopoly

characterisation   the way in which a writer creates characters so as to attract or repel our sympathy. Different kinds of literature have certain conventions of characterisation. In Jacobean drama there were many stock dramatic 'types' whose characteristics were familiar to the audience

chorus   Ancient Greek drama had a chorus, who usually acted as commentator rather than participant in the events, often with **ironic** insight

cliché   a widely used expression which, through overuse, has lost impact and originality

dramatic irony   occurs when the development of the plot means that the audience is in possession of more information about what is happening than some of the characters are

enjambment   the running over of a statement or sentence from one line of verse to the next

etymology   the study of the history and origins of words

eulogy   formal speech of high praise or commendation

foreshadowing   a literary technique whereby the author mentions events which are yet to be revealed in the narrative, either to increase dramatic tension, or to provide clues for the reader to guess what will happen next

homophone   a word which sounds identical to another but is spelt differently and has a different meaning (for example so/sew)

hyperbole   emphasis by exaggeration

hypermetric   a line of verse with more syllables than its pattern (for example **iambic pentameter**) allows

iambic pentameter   a line with five stressed beats, in a *ti-tum* weak-stress/strong-stress pattern

idiom   a characteristic mode of expression for a character

imagery   use of language to evoke sense-impressions

irony   saying one thing while meaning another

juxtaposition   the technique of placing two or more seemingly unrelated ideas next to each other in a text, creating meaning from the interaction of the differences and similarities between them

metaphor   a comparison of two things or ideas, which goes further than a **simile**, by fusing them together

Method   technique of acting based on the theories of Russian actor and director Konstantin Stanislavsky (1863–1938) in which ideas about the inner motivations and psychology of a character are the basis of the performance

motif   a recurring subject, theme or idea

nonce word   a word coined for a particular occasion

paradox   an apparently self-contradictory statement with an underlying meaning or truth beneath its superficial absurdity

pathos   moments in works of art which evoke strong feelings of pity are said to have this quality

pentameter   see **iambic pentameter**

Petrarch   fourteenth-century Italian poet who wrote sonnets about idealised, courtly and unrequited love, and used **paradoxes** such as 'icy heat'

pun   play on words, where two or more different meanings are drawn out of a single word for witty or comic effect

rhetoric   the art of speaking (and writing) effectively so as to persuade an audience

rhyming couplet   a pair of rhymed lines

rhythm   in English verse and prose the chief element of rhythm is the variation in levels of stress accorded to the syllables, in any stretch of language, creating a recurrent pattern of sounds, or a beat

satire   literature which examines vice and folly and makes them appear contemptible and ridiculous

simile   a figure of speech which compares two things using the words 'like' or 'as'

soliloquy   literally 'to speak alone' – hence a speech from a character when alone on stage, traditionally enabling him or her to express inner thoughts and feelings

sonnet   lyric poem consisting of fourteen rhyming lines

stichomythia   interchange of single lines in a dialogue, giving the impression of rapid but controlled arguments

symbol   something that represents something else by association

syntax   the arrangement of words in their appropriate forms and proper order, in order to achieve meaning and particular effects and emphases

trope   a figurative or metaphorical use of a word or expression, i.e. a word or phrase that is used in a sense that is not literal

verisimilitude   likeness to reality

TIMELINE

WORLD EVENTS	SHAKESPEARE'S LIFE	LITERARY EVENTS
		1513 Niccolò Machiavelli, *The Prince*
		1528 Castiglione, *Book of the Courtier*
		1531 *Gl'Ingannati* (source)
1534 Henry VIII breaks with Rome		
1556 Archbishop Cranmer burnt at the stake		
1558 Elizabeth I accedes to throne		
		1562 Lope de Vega, great Spanish dramatist, born
	1564 Born in Stratford-upon-Avon	
1570 Elizabeth I excommunicated		
	1576 James Burbage builds the first theatre in England, at Shoreditch	
1577 Francis Drake sets out on voyage round the world		
		c.1580 Sir Philip Sidney, *An Apologie for Poetrie*
		1581 Barnabe Riche, *Farewell to the Military Profession* (source)
	1582 Marries Anne Hathaway	
	1583 Their daughter, Susanna, is born	
1584 Raleigh's sailors land in Virginia		
	1585 Their twins, Hamnet and Judith, born	
1587 Execution of Mary Queen of Scots		
1588 The Spanish Armada defeated	**late 1580s–early 90s** Probably writes *Henry VI (Parts I, II, III)* and *Richard III*	**1588–9** Thomas Kyd, *The Spanish Tragedy*
		1590 Edmund Spenser, *Faerie Queene* (Books I–III)
1592 Plague in London closes theatres	**1592** Recorded as being a London actor and an 'upstart crow'	
	1592–4 Writes *The Comedy of Errors*	

WORLD EVENTS	SHAKESPEARE'S LIFE	LITERARY EVENTS
	1594 onwards Writes exclusively for the Lord Chamberlain's Men	
	pre-1595 *The Two Gentlemen of Verona, The Taming of the Shrew* and *Love's Labour's Lost* probably written	**1595** Death of William Painter, whose *Palace of Pleasure* provided sources for plots of many Elizabethan dramas
	c.1595 *Romeo and Juliet*	
1596 English raid on Cadiz	**1596–8** Hamnet dies; first performance, *The Merchant of Venice*	
	1598–9 Globe Theatre built at Southwark	
	1600 *A Midsummer Night's Dream, Much Ado about Nothing* and *The Merchant of Venice* printed in quartos	
	1600–1 *Hamlet*	
	1600–2 *Twelfth Night* written	
1603 Death of Queen Elizabeth I; accession of James Stuart	**1603 onwards** His company enjoys patronage of James I as the King's Men	
1605 Discovery of Guy Fawkes's plot	**1604** *Othello* performed **1605** First version of *King Lear*	**1605** Cervantes, *Don Quijote de la Mancha*
	1606 *Macbeth*	
	1606–7 *Antony and Cleopatra*	
	1608 The King's Men acquire Blackfriars Theatre for winter performances	
1610 William Harvey discovers circulation of blood		
	1611 *Cymbeline, The Winter's Tale* and *The Tempest* performed	
1612 Last burning of heretics in England		
	1613 Globe Theatre burns down	
	1616 Dies	
1618 Raleigh executed for treason; Thirty Years War begins in Europe		
	1623 First Folio of Shakespeare's works	

REVISION FOCUS TASK ANSWERS

TASK 1

The lasting impression left by this scene is of sad reflection rather than comic misunderstanding.

- There is literal misunderstanding – Orsino does not know Cesario is Viola, but in this scene it is not played for laughs.

- Viola genuinely believes her love to be in vain; after all, Orsino continues to profess his love for Olivia.

- Feste's song talks of a 'shroud of white' and a 'black coffin' – hardly comic images.

The impression of Orsino as self-obsessed and self-pitying is increased, not lessened, by what he says to Viola about love.

- Orsino says no woman could feel as deeply as he does, comparing his overwhelming feelings to the 'hungry' sea.

- Feste says, perhaps mockingly, 'Now the melancholy God of love protect thee.'

- Orsino ends the scene sending Viola off to Olivia with another love token, the ring, showing that he is set on the fruitless wooing of Olivia.

TASK 2

Malvolio's treatment at the hands of Feste and Sir Toby goes beyond reasonable revenge.

- It could be argued that in his treatment of Feste and Sir Toby, Malvolio is only doing his duty as a responsible steward of the house in a time of mourning.

- Malvolio has already been severely embarrassed, even humiliated by the fake love letter plot.

- However, his exit from the play, vowing revenge, suggests he has not been as damaged by events as might appear in this scene.

'Fool' is a particularly inappropriate term for Feste in this scene.

- Feste's ability to argue the finer points of religious and classical theories (such as Pythagoras's ideas) shows him to have learning.

- Feste demonstrates he is not just a serving clown to Olivia but has a mind of his own, effectively ignoring Sir Toby's instruction to 'deliver' Malvolio and speak to him in 'thine own voice'.

- He is able to switch seamlessly within the same sentence from his own voice to that of Sir Topas's, showing linguistic dexterity.

TASK 3

The overwhelming evidence of the play points towards Malvolio being an essentially tragic, rather than comic figure.

- Malvolio is an outsider – without obvious companions or friends.

- He is humiliated both in the 'gulling' scene and when imprisoned in the dungeon, and the love he expresses for Olivia may well be genuine, and will remain unrequited.

- The funniest moments of the play arise from his own flaws and ridiculous behaviour.

The most memorable dramatic moments of the play feature Malvolio. Without him the play's dramatic impact would be considerably lessened.

- Malvolio's actions act as a counterpoint to the blunt humour of Sir Toby, and a reminder to the audience of how pride comes before a fall.

- Act II Scene 5 (the finding of the letter) and Act III Scene 4 (Malvolio's appearance in yellow stockings) are the comic heart of the drama, both visually and linguistically, as the audience delights in Malvolio's self-love.

- Act IV Scene 2 (the dungeon scene) is both poignant and funny at the same time, and represents the moment when the mad world of Illyria is at its most 'topsy-turvy'.

TASK 4

Whilst 'mad' behaviour governs the play, by the end order and sanity are restored.

- There is 'madness' in Orsino's excessive love for Olivia; and her unnatural mourning for a dead brother.

- The ending restores order in terms of revealing Viola for who she is, reuniting her with her brother Sebastian, uncovering the plot against Malvolio, and matching the lovers.

- However, many of the seeds for mad or unreasonable behaviour remain, and Malvolio's exit threatens further disorder.

Madness is predominantly associated with love in the play.

- Characters refer to love as a kind of madness; Olivia saying that her quick love for Cesario is a kind of 'madness' making her 'as mad as he [Malvolio]' (III.4.14).

- Malvolio's 'madness' is the crime of expressing his feelings for Olivia.

- It can appear 'mad/strange' that a boy loves a man (Cesario and Orsino) and a woman loves a boy who is in fact a woman (Olivia and Cesario).

- In addition, there is the mad or reckless behaviour of others for love, such as Antonio who assists Sebastian out of love, despite putting his life at risk on enemy territory.

TASK 5

Shakespeare's comedies make powerful use of the plot device of twins for dramatic effect.

- Twins are used for plot effect in *The Comedy of Errors* and *Twelfth Night*.

- Contrast the perhaps over-contrived coincidences of two sets of identical twins in *The Comedy of Errors* with the more streamlined device of the later play with its one set of twins.

- Dramatic climax can be seen when the twins reunite, especially in *Twelfth Night* which has added poignancy as they believed each other dead.

The shipwrecks that open both *The Tempest* and *Twelfth Night* launch emotional after-effects that last throughout each play.

- The different types of shipwreck launch key storylines – the one a stimulus for a drama of revenge and atonement; the other a device to separate individuals so that they can pursue their own stories.

- *The Tempest*'s shipwreck is of a blighted ruler and a royal company; *Twelfth Night*'s of twins who separately fall in love. Both these are essential to the plays' development.

- In *The Tempest*, Prospero's magical redemption of the wrecked ship and sailors signals forgiveness, and ultimately abandonment of the island; in *Twelfth Night*, the arrival of Sebastian and Viola and their eventual marriages to Illyria's ruling Countess and Duke signal acceptance and fulfilment.

MARK SCHEME

Use this page to assess your answer to the **Worked task**, provided on pages 104–5.

Aiming for an A grade? Fulfil all the criteria below and your answer should hit the mark.*

> 'Shakespeare's enthronement of woman as queen of comedy is no mere accident ... these heroines have attributes of personality fitting them more certainly than men to shape the world toward happiness' (H. B. Charlton, *Shakespeare's Heroines and the Art of Happiness*). In your view how well does this statement apply to the female characters in *Twelfth Night*?

A01 — Articulate creative, informed and relevant responses to literary texts, using appropriate terminology and concepts, and coherent, accurate written expression.

- You make a range of clear, relevant points about women's roles within the play, their particular character traits, and comic impact on the drama.
- You write a balanced essay covering the three main female characters in the play – Maria, Olivia and Viola.
- You use a range of literary terms correctly, e.g. **aside**, **metaphor**, **pun**, **syntax**.
- You write a clear introduction, outlining your thesis, and provide a clear conclusion.
- You signpost and link your ideas together clearly about women's comedic impact.

A02 — Demonstrate detailed critical understanding in analysing the ways in which structure, form and language shape meanings in literary texts.

- You explain the techniques and methods Shakespeare uses to present the 'attributes' of women and link these to the key idea of establishing contentment and bringing joy to the drama.
- You may discuss, for example, the way that Maria's lively mind instigates the 'gulling' of Malvolio and how this brings pleasure both to audience and actors within the drama.
- You explain in detail how your examples affect meaning, e.g. Viola's 'I am not that I play' allowing Elizabethan audiences both to delight in the transgression of gender norms, and yet find comfort in the conventions of mask and disguise.
- You might explore how the setting – the leisurely court, and close community of Illyria – allow for the expression of female independence.

A03 — Explore connections and comparisons between different literary texts, informed by interpretations of other readers.

- You make relevant links between Shakespeare's treatment of his heroines in *Twelfth Night* with his presentation of them in similar comedies, where appropriate.
- You incorporate and comment on critics' views of women's roles in the play, and the extent to which these underline the assertion in the title, or challenge it.
- You assert your own independent view clearly.

A04 — Demonstrate understanding of the significance and influence of the contexts in which literary texts are written and received.

- You explain how relevant aspects of social, literary and historical contexts of *Twelfth Night* are significant when interpreting ideas related to female identity and comic impact.

For example, you may discuss:
- Literary context – the role of the Fool, and the extent to which it/he is usurped by Maria and/or Viola in different ways.
- Historical context – the impact of Puritanism on the theatre, and the extent to which the female characters are aligned against its representative in the play, Malvolio.
- Social context – the role of women in Elizabethan society more generally, and the degree to which they were constrained or liberated by marriage contracts.

* This mark scheme gives you a broad indication of attainment, but check the specific mark scheme for your paper/task to ensure you know what to focus on.